To Brian,
Best Wishes!

91 BRAVO MEDIC

A Memoir of the

Second Korean War

George Strejcek

To the United States Army Medical Corps Past Present and Future

The Living and the Dead

I have not always been wrong about the future of events and if you will permit me, I shall inscribe some of these words as my testament because I should like to be held accountable for them in years which I shall not see.

Winston Churchill

The events in this memoir happened.   Only the names and locations have been altered.

Special Thanks to Elizabeth Cowan Strejcek for editing and support.

Explanation of terms at end.

Printed by Createspace, an Amazon.com Company

Chapter One

April 1968: The OD turned to me and said, "We just got a call from the 728th MPs; there has been some sort of *accident* near Bupyong. A group of hysterical soldiers are saying: "The Chief is gone. He fell off a bridge! Get the ambulance driver and head over there! Private!"

Daily, the ambulance driver, was driving too fast. The unpaved road was filled with potholes. We could see lights in the distance. Kimchee Creek was easy to follow. It wound around the paddy fields approximately parallel to the road. The ambulance was not built for off-road use and I bumped my head hard on the roof. We followed the creek in the general direction of the faint lights. Pulling off the road we stopped and approached the MPs. Must be serious. The senior policeman was a SFC.

"What happened sergeant?"

The MP shifted on his feet and said, "Seems some drunk GIs got lost out here in the dark. They found the railroad tracks and decided to follow them back to Bupyong. Didn't stop when they reached the bridge and attempted to cross it in the dark. One of them fell off. He is probably directly under the span." Turning to me, he said, "You'd better get moving." I looked at the sergeant and asked him if he would help in the search. "Not my job, Private. You have got a flashlight and a driver."

I did not know the depth of Kimchee Creek. This was not your hometown swimming hole. It smelled of stale urine and feces. I unlaced my boots in the event the water was over my head. Stepped into the creek and headed toward the bridge. It was quite high, at least three stories and resting on substantial concrete supports. The water initially was not deep, maybe up to my knees. It was a good fifty yards to the pilings. On I went, slipping occasionally on the slimy river bottom. Fortunately, there was no detectable current. Reaching the bridge I looked around for a few minutes finding nothing. Moving around to the third piling I saw something white just beneath the surface. It looked like a sheet of white paper. I reached down and got my hand on the collar of a jacket. The Chief was face down with his arms splayed out as if he had just completed a swan dive. I called out to the MP's that I found him.

"Bring him back" said the SFC.

I tried to move the corpse but I couldn't lift him. Too heavy. Dead weight. I called back to the MPs, "Need some help here, can't budge him!"

The MPs called back, "Not our job, get your driver to help!"

Daily weighed in at about 145 pounds. I was not sure we could lift the chief who was over 200. I could hear splashing and saw him approaching with a stretcher.

The MPs told me, "Stay where you are. The CID is coming" A criminal investigation? There is no crime here just a terrible accident. I did not want to remain in this fetid water until the spooks showed up. Ten minutes elapsed, by this time I was shaking from the cold. The CID men arrived took their photos and departed.

"OK, Daily, let's get the Chief back to the hospital." I do not remember the trip back only that I talked to myself a little and we were met by a contingent of nurses and physicians.

The body was placed flat on the floor of the emergency room. The chief's hip did not look right. It was misaligned, probably broken. First Sergeant Goetz looked me straight in the eye and said, "Why didn't you try to use the ambu bag?" Was this idiot serious? At least twenty minutes elapsed between the initial call from the 728 MPs and our arrival on the scene, plus another ten minutes searching.

"No, Sergeant, I could tell he was dead and was standing in at least three feet of water."

"There will be an investigation private!"

****

February 4, 1968

Oakland Army terminal was not welcoming. The facility was not designed to house animals much less people. It looked like a warehouse really or a series of warehouses that had somehow been renovated to house overseas bound troops. The only amenities were toilets: nine of them for several thousand men. The problem was there were no flights to Vietnam. The biggest air terminals, Bien Hoa and Tan San Nhut, were under rocket attack. No arrivals, no departures.

I had to check in with a middle aged, balding sergeant holding a clip board with a sheaf of papers. Just ahead of me a nineteen year old private with a smirk on his face was checking in. "You are two weeks late returning from terminal leave, Private," said the reddening sergeant. "You are in trouble!"

"Really?" Replied the calm private, "What are you going to do? Send me to Vietnam?"

"OK wise guy, move out. We will call you."

How long I remained in Oakland is gone... two days, three days, no longer sure. Sometime during the third day another sergeant appeared with another clipboard. "Who would like to go to Korea?" We need 11 Bravos and 91 Bravos!" I volunteered immediately. "You people are going to Ft. Lewis." It took another four hours or so to cut orders. Farewell, Oakland, Hello, Seattle!

San Francisco was impressive. The hills were filled with one and two story stucco houses painted in beautiful pastels. I did not want to leave. The pilot of the 727 was very considerate; flying up the Pacific coast he flew low and gave us a running commentary on what we were viewing. I guess he realized that for some of us it would be the last view of the U.S.A. It was a memorable trip.

Ft. Lewis was another surprise. The two-story

yellow barracks were still heated by coal stoves. Behind each barrack was a cement coal bin and an enlisted man was detailed to shovel the stuff into a scuttle and feed the fire. The acrid smell of the burning coal suffused with the aroma of pine.

McChord Air Force Base was a short distance from Ft. Lewis. We loaded aboard the DC-8 and waited and waited. About forty-five minutes later the pilot came on the PA. He cleared his throat. "Gentlemen, we are being rerouted. There are Anti-American demonstrations at Narita, therefore, we will not be landing in Japan. Our initial stop will be Honolulu, then Wake Island, Guam and Kimpo, South Korea. We expect the flight will take about twenty-three hours."

****

February 12, 1968

The door opened on the DC-8 and we disembarked onto the tarmac. It was cold, about 25 degrees. We walked over to the terminal and stood in line. Ushered into an adjoining room we were told to drop our pants. Drop our pants? "Gentlemen," intoned the Sergeant, "Welcome to Korea. This is Asia, men. You are going to get a gamma globulin shot to prevent hepatitis. This is a requirement!" It was two shots: one in each buttock and it hurt. We boarded blue buses and left Kimpo for ASCOM, a replacement Depo. ASCOM, or ashcan as it was known during the war, was a barren piece of ground about twelve miles outside of Seoul. It was vintage 1950's Army. Nothing but Quonset huts.

After about two hours, a sergeant walked through the door with a clipboard. "Sirkin and Collins come with me, you are assigned to the 642 hospital."

"Welcome gentlemen," stated the company commander. "I am Captain Jonas. We are glad to see you. The hospital is understaffed due to the Vietnam War. Sirkin you will be assigned to the OR, Collins you go to Ward C-22. Post-Op. First Sergeant Goetz will assign you a billet. Dismissed"

Barracks 222 was Spartan. There were twenty beds with a kerosene space heater in the center. Peter thought to himself, better than an air mattress or worse: in the field. There were several men sound asleep and the barrack was mostly empty. A Korean was busily ironing some fatigues. "Hello, GI. You sleep here. Wall locker there. Put in clothes. I iron. You pay end of month. OK?"

I sat down and removed a bottle of Scotch from my duffel bag. A souvenir of Guam, it didn't break. I must have dozed off, jet lag and the whiskey. I awoke to the sound of a loud cackle. A short dark soldier stood above me laughing. "Welcome to short-timer heaven. It ain't much but it's better than the DMZ or Vietnam!" He laughed again, it was a peculiar laugh, half manic. "You have to join me for a tour of our USO club. Up north they call it the Turkey Ranch. Here it's called Sinchon or Little City. Sin City we call it. Quite a place" He laughed again.

The next day was my introduction to the 642 hospital. It was a series of Quonset huts joined together by cold passages. Some of it was actually below ground. Due to the hilly terrain if you exited through one of the many fire doors you had to walk uphill to reach the helipad. Sgt. Helborn was a slow talking Alabamian. He smiled when he saw me. "You RA or U.S. son?" I said I was drafted. "Well, there's plenty to do here. Lots of cleaning; putting up instrument packs. You see those big stainless steel tanks?"

"Yes, Sergeant. Large autoclaves."

"Right. We keep them busy. This is the closest field hospital to the DMZ we get everything here, including some civilians. You will start cleaning instruments. Thoracotomy trays are the largest. You scrub all the instruments and place them on the trays according to the list here." He handed me a plastic covered sheet listing the hemostats, retractors and knives used on the tray. I never heard the term scalpel used in any context in thirteen months. They were always called knives.

The doctors in the 642 were an eclectic lot from all over the lower forty-eight. One was the grandson of a Russian nobleman: a staunch anti-communist. The most impressive was a former full-back at Baylor University who was an orthopedic surgeon and an all-around nice guy. The lifer medics were generally competent and cheerful. Tom Grimaldi was the hospital "character"; loud but not profane, intelligent but not well-schooled. I was to find out later he was a master poker-player. Unbeatable!

I continued to put up instrument packs for several weeks. Sgt. Helborn approached me one day and said, "Scrub up this morning, you are going to the operating room." A scrub nurse generally passes instruments from a tray to the surgeon. Enlisted people were called operating room technicians, performing, in effect, the job of an RN. Grimaldi was an OR tech. As I came to know him, there were really two Toms: the on-duty Tom and the off-duty Grimaldi. Off-duty Grimaldi was a wild man, always up to something. On-duty he became another entity: entirely serious and subdued.

On the third morning, a gunshot victim arrived at the hospital. The sergeant was in his mid-thirties and apparently shot himself. He was unconscious and ashen. The bullet from a .45 automatic had entered his chest slightly below his left nipple missing the heart and exiting his back. A portion of a rib was protruding from the wound. It was rectangular in shape and exuded foamy red blood: a collapsed lung. The General Surgeon, Captain Stanfield was assigned to the case. By reputation he was the best thoracic surgeon in the hospital. Little anesthesia was used. The patient was breathing shallowly, his eyes wide open. Dr. Stanfield explained exactly what he was doing. This was a major procedure. The inventor of the .45 automatic knew what he was doing. The electric bovey cautery gave off the aroma of burnt chicken. The small bleeders are cauterized again and again. The patient was still in hemorrhage but Captain Stanfield would not give up. He expertly tied off the smaller vessels. Before it was over the Sergeant was operated on twice. It took him three days to die. They couldn't stem the bleeding. Later an NCO came to collect his effects. Why did it happen? Apparently, a "Dear John Letter."

"Pete", said Tom Grimaldi, "How long you been here now? couple of weeks?"

"Yeah, about that."

"It's about time you get initiated. You've got to go to the club".

"Been there, not much. Just pool tables."

"No, not the USO club - the Showboat Club!"

"They warned us about that place first week, said it should be avoided. VD down there."

Tom cackled, "Not as long as you keep your fly buttoned, fella."

The Showboat Club was only about one-hundred yards beyond the ASCOM compound. Sinchon, or little city, was a typical storefront affair located near the many Army bases in Korea. It resembled a strip mall with stores and clubs catering to Americans as well as the locals. The clubs for GIs were named the Silver Dollar, Showboat, San Francisco and the like. There was a narrow creek that ran in back of the clubs, it was called Kimchee. The streets were unpaved and very slippery after rain storms. It closely resembled Deadwood, South Dakota during the 19th century. We entered. It was dimly lit with music blaring through large speakers: "Well, I heard it through the grape vine. Just about to lose my mind." The latest music from stateside. The girls were lounging at the tables smoking and looking for clients. "Sophia," yelled Tom followed by his manic cackle. Sophia covered her face with her hand and looked away. "They all give themselves names after Hollywood stars," said Tom. "We have Marilyns, Tammies, Natalies, you name it!" Sophia recovered from her embarrassment and was smiling now. Apparently Tom was a favorite.

"Just how many of these 'ladies' are you familiar with?" asked Pete.

Another loud cackle, "A few!"

"What can you order in the way of liquid refreshment, Tom?" asked Pete.

"Only bottled beer, OB is Korean not bad," said Tom. The waiter approached us with two bottles. "Pay now," said Tom. "They don't keep a tab." Tom turned in his seat and motioned to Sophia. "We dance baby-san?" Sophia jumped out of her seat with a big smile. What followed was not a dance but a performance. Tom kept time with the music by clapping loudly and laughing. The patrons began to watch the show in earnest, they couldn't believe it! I couldn't believe it! If the Rockettes had showed up at the Showboat, they could not have garnered this much attention. How long the performance continued, I no longer remember. I do remember going to the rest room. On the door was emblazoned in large letters. "IF YOU TAKE A GIRL HOME BE SURE TO WEAR A CONDOM, IT IS THE BEST WAY TO PREVENT VD." Under this was a pencil comment in small letters. "Now you tell me!"

The 642 hospital staff was competent. The physicians were graduates of top notch medical schools and dedicated professionals. Since Korea was not considered a combat zone, at least south of the Imjin River, many had brought their wives and children. The nurses were a different matter. Some of them came out of a sense of patriotism. There was a shooting war going on a few thousand miles away. Some were looking for adventure. Some were looking for potential husbands and others were looking for sexual experiences. They didn't have to wait long. The best of the lot was a major. Major Dimick was regular Army with nine years in the service. Plainly speaking it was impossible to hide her charms, even in the bulky woolens she routinely wore.

Like the line in Stalag 17, "I want her even if she wears galoshes!"
I am sure she was competent, otherwise she would not have been
wearing the gold leaves of a major. The problem was she could
not perform the basic tasks of a floor nurse. She approached an
injection as one might throw a dart in an English pub. Overhand
and tentatively. Apparently she found it abhorrent to pierce the
flesh of a human being. One day, early on, she was visiting a
ward attempting to start an IV. Veins can be peculiar, some roll
around like soda straws. The flesh has to be drawn tightly by a
gentle pull and the needle placed at a shallow angle. I was
delivering a patient from the recovery room and happened to
glance over at the unfolding scene. The Major was bending over
the terrified young man attempting to do the deed. She was turning
red. I walked over and inquired sweetly, "May I help, Major?" She
almost surrendered the needle when she noticed it was a Private
attempting to render aid. To my great surprise she turned over the
IV set to me, and I placed the needle. First time. Instead of
harboring a grudge or marking me as a trouble-maker she smiled
and thanked me. Quickly excusing herself. Her smile was genuine
and as beautiful as the rest of the package. I guess, at that point,
Pete was hooked, but so was every other male within shouting
distance.

Passing by the emergency room one afternoon, I
overheard a muted conversation and loud laughter. Inquisitiveness
overcame caution. I walked in and inquired, "What's so funny?"

"Specialist Guest has clap."

"What's so unusual about a case of gonorrhea?" asked
Pete.

"It's where he got it!"

"Where?" I inquired.

"His mouth!" More gales of laughter.

"You mean he had oral sex with one of the ville
prostitutes?"

"Yep." C'est La Guerre!

Each physician had his own peculiarities. Captain Stanfield was a talker during a procedure he would explain what he was doing to the nurses and medics in the OR. It was as if he was surrounded by interns and he was giving the do's and don'ts of surgery. "Do Not Cut HERE on the abdomen. Important nerves just about here!" The man was incredible; a genius. He was also one of the most genuine and caring men I ever met. His specialty was open heart surgery.

Count Leo Tolstoy as Dr.Stoloff was called was slow and methodical. Not given to excessive talk, Stoloff was competent but overly deliberate. Our urologist made no secret of the fact he thought the Vietnam War was a travesty. Well educated and well spoken, he refused to hold his tongue at the officer's club. Physicians in the Army were given considerable latitude regarding their personal opinions and did not suffer any retribution. We were short of experienced and talented people. Vietnam was the main concern in the military.

****

Easter Sunday 1968
The call came out on foot. The CQ runner burst through the door just past 11:00 P.M. "All O.R. techs to the emergency room! Mass casualty alert!" Pete and Tom awoke with a start. Mass casualties are only called in a war zone. Most medics were sleeping. We got dressed and ran down to the hospital. Things were moving quickly. The distant "Whap Whap" of the Huey dust-off could be faintly discerned. What the hell! Mass casualty situation! Has the second Korean War started? The senior OR Techs ran in the hospital and disappeared. Sirkin being a floater and new to the hospital was told to stand by and help unload the chopper. The helo' flared and settled on the helipad. The door slid open and a crew member beckoned with his left hand. I ran up to the door and grabbed two handles of the stretcher. It was shackled to the wall

of the Huey and was quickly released by the crewman. The soldier was unconscious with his eyes wide open. He looked to be alive. Two other men helped me run the stretcher to the hospital entrance. A Gurney was waiting. I released my grip on the stretcher and it came away moist and red. I was not in the OR during the procedure. Dr. Stanfield was awakened and he cracked the chest of the wounded man. A bullet had entered the soldier's chest and exited the back. It had pierced his left ventricle. I later learned that Stanfield had operated on the infantryman without a surgical gown or routine scrub. He entered the hospital wearing khaki trousers and tee shirt, sewed up the defect and defibrillated the heart, but the stitches would not hold and pressure was never restored in the circulatory system. He was essentially D.O.A. According to a senior medic, his entire blood volume was pooled in his thoracic cavity. Another man was killed that night, two others were wounded and survived.

Tensions were palpable in mid-April. The death of M.L. King further divided racial tensions in the Far East. Some idiot raised a confederate flag at Bien Hoa in Vietnam. The ville' was off- limits for three days until things cooled down.

Two months in Korea with eleven to go. Pete was ashamed of himself. Twenty-four years old and still a virgin! He was afraid of women or rejection or both. It was high time to do something about it. It was dark when he made it to a club on the far reaches of Bupyong. He did not want to be seen because he was too embarrassed. Ducking in "The Happening", a seldom visited club with fewer amenities than the Showboat, he sat down and ordered a drink. He glanced around the club and spotted a girl in a black sheath dress. She seemed bigger than most of those he had seen and quite attractive. He got up and walked over to her table. She was beautiful, tall and well-proportioned. He felt his blood rising. "You want take me home G.I.?" Not very subtle but who cared? She led me though a winding mud path to what looked like a tea house. Inside there were sliding panels of wood and paper. The cubicles were small about ten by eight feet. There was a padding of feet after I gave my 1,000 won to the Madam. I turned around and watched the panel open slightly and a pack of cigarettes was thrown in by the old woman. They landed on the floor. I bent over and picked them up. When I turned around, she was already naked. She wore nothing under the black sheath. Her body was perfect: full breasts, large for a Korean, and beautiful hips descending to black pubic hair. I must have turned red because she chuckled slightly. She got into the bed and beckoned me. Suddenly I went limp literally. I just stared. Minutes must have passed. She said, "You no can make love?" With that I grabbed her breast. "Sangama!" she blurted. I found out later that meant a vulgar person. By this time I was hard. I peeled the condom on. She spread her legs. I attempted to mount her. I could not enter her. She said something under her breath and grabbed my penis. Finally, she turned her head slightly and smiled. I believe the smile was for some G.I. she must have liked. Not for me. In any event, she seemed to enjoy it. If not for me, no problem. So this was it. **Raw Sex**. Nothing to it! I was afraid of the ladies for nothing and got a genuine smile from a pro. She removed the condom for me and handed it back. "Souvenir", she said.

In the latter part of April, the Jewish Doctors began to arrive. It was like a Diaspora; so many so fast. It took me years to figure out why. Jews must have posed some imaginary security risk. Remember the Jewish, Communist, Liberal Conspiracy? In any event, they were quiet (apolitical), professional and spent many off hours in the extensive hospital medical library. Also, they did not engage in any off-hours hanky-panky like most of the enlisted men and some of the physicians.

I was transferred to ward duty about this time, and left the OR only to return one night during an emergency. I had no serious problems in the hospital but this was not to last. Ward work was deadly dull for the most part; internal medicine was especially routine. The hepatitis ward was also my responsibility. Some of the hepatitis patients were in a very poor state. Yellow jaundice is well named. In extreme cases, the white of the eye turned mustard yellow. There was little that could be done for these patients other than bed rest and good nutrition. In several months they could be released for light duty. Some of the patients liked hospital life and did not want to leave. Others wanted out immediately. Urine was routinely checked for bilirubin content. A nurse once caught two men switching their urine samples. The malingerers were never punished.

In the neighboring ward, which I covered, there were also some interesting cases. One senior Sergeant had been in Moscow with Averill Harriman on a diplomatic mission in 1942. His reward for almost thirty years of faithful service to the United States? Infantry duty on the DMZ. Physically, at the age of fifty-one, his body could not take patrol work. How this was allowed to happen, I never knew. One man who was hospitalized for high blood pressure was another Master Sergeant named Martin (The recipient of a Purple Heart and Bronze Star in the 30th Infantry Division). I asked him what his most memorable experience was in WWII. He stated the defense of Mortain in Normandy. The Germans had attempted to flank Patton's break out at Avaranches in August 1944. The 30th division fought to contain the Germans and prevent the attack from succeeding. The wounded from his company were left on the side of the road when the Germans made a temporary breakthrough. Later in the day, they regained the town and discovered the Nazis had systematically cut the throats of the wounded Americans. The look on Sergeant Martin's face was one I will never forget.

I met in my Army career one horse soldier: an African American who joined the cavalry at Ft. Riley Kansas in 1938. He was past retirement, but was kept in for medical reasons. He was suffering from terminal syphilis. The condition associated with the tertiary stage of the disease was sarcodosis. His skin was literally sloughing off in strips resembling serious burns. The pain must have been excruciating but he bore it without complaint. Only the facial expressions I witnessed bore witness to his agony.

****

The days passed and I did not return to the ville'. I felt guilty about betraying myself and compromising my own values, but finally, the conquering hormones took over. I returned to the "Happening" and looked for the young lady. She was gone, where to I never knew. Disappointed and lonely I went back to the barracks and pondered my next move.

There was a formation called in the small hospital movie theatre one day to explain some new protocol which I can no longer remember. I was late in arriving. Figuring I would announce my arrival with a flourish, I yelled, "Ten-Hut!" which was normally used to announce the arrival of the company commander. One hundred and ten men jumped to rigid attention. I sauntered up to the front of the theatre and sat down with a smile on my face. Big mistake! I paid dearly for my effrontery, but from that day on I was a marked man. Private Sirkin's name began to appear on the Extra Duty Roster with alarming frequency. Also my pass card mysteriously disappeared from the wall cabinet. I asked about it and a smirking clerk in the orderly room said, "We'll make a new one." The joke was on me. After about a week of this no pass routine, I walked into the orderly room and went straight to the company commander's office and asked, "Where is my pass?" No salute and no asking for permission to speak. The Captain leaped to his feet, turning purple and said, "Who the hell do you think you are, Private? Get the Hell out of my office!" The chance of getting that "dear" pass back was receding like a mirage.

****

Early May 1968

It was well after 9:00 P.M. I was going to get out of that compound with or without a pass. The ten foot high cyclone fence topped with barbed wire loomed out of the darkness. What was I going to do once I got out? I figured I could get a drink or something and get back before curfew. Up the cyclone fence I went. I was just topping the barbed wire when I heard a loud, "Halt!" and what sounded like the racking of a shotgun. It was. I stared down the barrel of a 12 gauge riot gun in the hands of a determined Korean guard. A situation like this concentrates your thoughts like little else this side of paradise. If the Korean disliked Americans he could have cranked off a round and gotten away with it. Fortunately, he was saner or more sober than yours truly. I knew I was in serious trouble. They had me but good. I jumped off the fence as meekly as I could with both hands raised. Off to the 728 MP Shack. There were two cells at the MP station. No bars just cyclone fencing as a barrier. Who would try to escape? I had already seen the results of getting shot with a Colt .45. The First Sergeant arrived about forty-five minutes later. I don't exactly remember what Goetz said but my mother and relatives would be embarrassed. I faced the Company Commander early the next morning. My demeanor must have mirrored my contrition because he appeared to be trying hard to mask a smile. "What's the idea Private? Trying for a little R&R?" The First Sergeant seemed genuinely upset; the Captain less so. "I see by your records that you have over three years of college, is that correct?"

"Yes Sir."

"You realize you could have been shot and killed don't you?"

"Yes Sir."

"Are you on duty today, Sirkin?"

"Yes Sir."

"Well, get going. You are confined to Barracks 'til further notice. Dismissed!"

I waited and waited. Three days passed. I found out from one of the orderly room clerks that a summary court martial was being considered. But no paper work had been typed up. On or about the fourth day, a runner summoned me to the orderly room.

The First Sergeant cast me a baleful look and sat down. I heard the words, "Send him in." I walked in and saluted. "I am not going to court martial you, Sirkin." The blood drained out of my face. "You are restricted to your barrack for two weeks and you will be fined $50. If you agree to this you must sign the Article 15." Did I agree? Like Jonah being spit out of the whale. I signed the document. "Any more attempts like this to leave the base without permission and I am going to see to it that you serve time in the Eighth Army stockade, understood?"

"Yes Sir." Much later I learned that the physicians at the Officer's club upon hearing the story laughed and two even applauded. It seems that I was providing some comic relief to the hospital staff. About a week later, Dr. Yablonski passed me in a corridor and exclaimed, "I am personally sitting in on your court martial, Pete." Pete? I had never even met the man. I noticed a strange change in the demeanor of the staff. People looked at me as though they were viewing an apparition. Nearly shot by a Korean guard evidently was a first!

****

The rotation system in effect during the Vietnam War was predicated on a twelve or thirteen month tour. Twelve months in Vietnam, thirteen in Korea. The comings and goings of staff made it hard to keep track. Major Dimick was gone, so was the company commander. Major Dimick passed me in the corridor during out-processing and made a point of asking me to look her up in Washington after I left the service. She was going to Walter Reed. 'Walter Wonderful' as it was known in those days.

It was about this time that I made the acquaintance of Nathan Rosen. He was a Spec. Six; essentially a Staff Sergeant without stripes. I never understood why the identical rank necessitated a different set of chevrons. The difference lay in the ability to give orders. A "hard striper" was somehow granted more cachet than a "specialist". During one evening bull-session, I asked Nate why he decided to make the Army a career. He said something that I always remembered. "My father made the decision for me."

"How so?" I asked. It stemmed from the fact the elder Rosen, a cloth cutter in the garment district in New York, was an ardent Zionist. He wanted his seventeen-year-old son to go to Palestine and help out the nascent Zionist army the Hagganah. Nate refused. He considered himself an American even though he could speak Yiddish fluently. After months of badgering, he ran away from home and joined the U.S. Army. He trained as an enlisted medic and was sent to Germany in 1947 as part of the American Occupation Force. The company he was attached to was in a small town outside Munich. After less than a month he was being singled out by the townspeople as a Jew. The Burger Meister of the town went to his company commander and stated, "We do not want this Jew in our town!" Incredibly PFC Rosen was transferred immediately to France. He was separated from service in 1950, disgusted and disillusioned by the anti-Semitism suffered in the Army. His father got him a job in the garment industry. He married and had a son. In 1955, his only child died from scarlet fever and his marriage fell apart. With few career options, he reentered the army. Nate was never really accepted by his fellow NCOs and was the archetype 'odd man out.'

For a homely man, Nate managed to pick up women quickly. He found a steady Korean girlfriend who made it known she wanted a ticket to the U.S.A. He did not want to get married again. How to remedy the situation? Get pregnant. Which she did. The new company commander, Sideburns, was faced with a very pregnant and very angry honey demanding money for breach of promise, and potential child support. Legal counsel was sought and the JAG officer stated the woman had no case due to the fact she was a registered prostitute.

The powers that be had let me off the hook with a slap on the wrist. But the Company Sergeants were in no forgiving mood. I was on the extra duty roster all the time. They controlled who did what among the enlisted men. The standard punishment was CQ runner. Buck Turgidson states in "Dr. Strangelove", "The Air Force Never Sleeps" The same can be said for all the other branches. I ran. This was an all night gig from about 8:00P.M to 7:00 A.M. If an emergency arose, it was generally initiated by a telephone call. The CQ runner ran to the appropriate barrack or officer hooch and awakened the proper person from his slumber. There were no telephones to the barracks in 1968, so all messages were delivered in person. The CQ runner was allowed to sleep on a mattress in the orderly room if nothing was happening, so it was possible to get sufficient rest.

****

July 21, 1968

The phone rang about 1:00 A.M. I awoke with a start. Sgt. Turpin was responding to a call from Camp Casey. "Sirkin, they want to alert the hospital. Firefight on the DMZ, wounded inbound. They say whole blood is needed. Get moving! The O.D is on the phone in the hospital." The closest Barrack to the E.R. housed the mess hall staff. Not thinking, I ran there first, switched on the light and yelled, "Get up, there has been a firefight on the DMZ we need blood!" What happened next is something I will never forget. No complaints, no curses, no "Go to Hells!" The men were all draftees, all minority and they got dressed and went to the emergency room silently without complaint.

Sgt. Turpin said, "Go to the emergency room and make sure we get at least eight pints of whole blood!" Off I went. Incredibly there were only two people visible on duty. What remained of the night staff were already preparing the ORs for patients.

I looked for the empty infusion sets. Fortunately, they were visible in a glass fronted stainless steel cabinet. The mess men were standing in the receiving room silent. I said, "OK, I can take four right now!" They all began moving toward the ER door. I directed three of the men to the available examining tables. No fumbling, I started three blood bags and was preparing a forth when the lights went out. Jesus! What a time for a power failure! Fortunately, within five minutes the lights came back on. The base was equipped with huge Diesel generators to supply the hospital with electricity in the event the local power grid failed. The next week the same thing happened, another ambush several dead and wounded. I slept through that one.

The clubs began to beckon about this time. The Showboat Club was loaded with GIs. I sat down and ordered the usual OB beer. A bargirl in a red dress approached me and said, "How about it, Mogo-Da?" I realized mogo-da meant dick-eater. But I figured, what the hell. I followed her down the muddy street. The twisting path led us to a large weathered wooden door. She shared a home with a Korean family. The high cement wall surrounding the compound was topped by broken glass bottles embedded in cement. Inside was a large enclosed courtyard. We entered her hootch through a sliding wood and paper door. I searched my pocket for the condom I thought I had but came up empty. It didn't take long. "You pays your money and takes your chances," as the saying goes. I lost. Three days later I experienced the usual pain on urination. Off to the ER. for treatment. The Army awards medals for killing people but never acknowledges the part sex plays in military organizations. General Petraeus was widely lauded for his performance in Iraq which involved the deaths of more than 100,000 civilians. But when he screwed his biographer his career was over. In WWII venereal disease was a court-martial offense. In the sixties you were simply denied promotion. This was the situation in Korea and Vietnam. After taking the cure, I hatched a plan to help my fellow Troops with their "problems." Opiates in the military outside of a combat zone were strictly controlled. Penicillin was not considered a controlled substance so it could be purloined without notice. I became the "lady with the lamp." Florence Nightingale could not have won a popularity contest against me. What started the thought process was our barrack helper. Scottie was our houseboy, after a weekend of revelry with the local lovelies he came down with the drip. After the conclusion of the day shift he approached me and said. "Pete, you help me?' Without so much as a 'by your leave', he whipped out his tiny member which seemed to be in grave distress. "I can't help you, Scottie. If word gets out that I am treating Koreans without authorization, I would be in serious trouble." The dejection was palpable, he lowered his head and walked away. It was then I began to help myself to the abundant supply of Uncle Sam's antibiotics. Sometimes I injected it into myself (an ounce of prevention is worth a pound of cure), sometimes, into infantrymen. Why I wasn't caught, mystifies me still after forty-six years. The Manhattan project never had such a code of silence, or the mafia for that matter.

****

By 1968 it was becoming apparent that the Vietnam War was not going well. As stated earlier the overseas tour in the Far-East was at least one year. After the Pueblo was seized in January 1968, tours in Korea were extended by months. The only assured way of getting back to the states was in an aluminum box or very serious wounds. We began to see in Korea so called "profiles." These were men with problems serious enough to get them out of combat, but not serious enough for a medical discharge. Uncle Sam was feign to give out medical discharges. These cost money, tax-payer money! Death in service of your country only cost $10,000, while disability benefits could run into the hundreds of thousands. My first experience with "physical profiles" was Fernando Reyes. This poor kid was not even a U.S. citizen. Somehow he wound up 1A with his local draft board. He was gainfully employed in a vegetable market, paying taxes and living in Houston, Texas. He was drafted in 1967 and wound up in the 25th tropic Lightning Division. This division was heavily engaged in fighting in 1967. Fernando was standing on a rice paddy dike shooting at the enemy. Air Force tactical air was called in and napalm struck the advancing Viets with liquid fire. He spoke with awe regarding the bravery of the NVA. "They were on fire and still trying to shoot at us." Several weeks later, his unit came under attack and this time an Apache helicopter was called in to provide support. Once again standing on a dike he was firing at the enemy and a rocket from the Apache prematurely exploded and a large fragment entered his abdomen and exited his back, narrowly missing his spine. He had ugly scars front and back from the abdominal surgery. A medical board rule ruled him unfit for combat as he had lost at least three feet of his small intestine. Did this rate a medical discharge? Not on your life. Off to Korea.

Again, as a result of my permanent placement on the extra duty roster, I was tasked to exercise some of these men. Fernando was about 5'10" in height with long legs. Not being a physical therapist I decided running would be therapeutic. Off we went, around the base perimeter. Nando, as he liked to be called, did surprisingly well easily keeping up with me. Problems arose at meal time. The damage must have been significant as after eating a light meal he experienced pain. I would often see him grasping his stomach making faces that evidenced serious discomfort. Not being a medic, Nando was charged with washing floors and sweeping up in the orderly room. He also worked at the motor pool. I never found out what happened, but one day he simply disappeared. Gone. The story went that he got into an argument with the company Sergeant Major. One thing led to another and Nando told his eminence to fuck himself. End of story. I hope he had a long life.

It was often said the most dangerous missile in WWII was a two and one half ton truck driven by a nineteen year old private. I would add something even more dangerous, a nineteen year old inebriated private driving a jeep. Abner came into the hospital on a stretcher: unconscious. Apparently he was driving too fast at night and missed a curve. The jeep continued in a straight line, Abner made the curve sans jeep. He landed in a sitting position on one of the only paved roads in the vicinity of the 642. The anus of a human being is only several inches in diameter. Abner's was split wide open six inches. He had received a colostomy and was now defecating in a plastic bag. The anus had to be stuffed with iodine soaked gauze to prevent infection. Guess who got the job? I thought my bedside manner was good enough under these conditions, but Abner was not appreciative. In fact he was very angry with me. I tried to fob my task onto one of the nurses. No dice, rank had its privileges. After about a week or so, Abner was evacuated to the States. He had a serious long term problem. I forgive his profanity.

I seemed to get all the prize winners. It was unusual to get Korean nationals in the 642 evacuation hospital you had to be politically well-connected. Korea at that time was not a democracy. It was ruled by a military cabal led by Park-Chung-Hee. Park ruled with an iron fist. Some years later he was assassinated by his own generals. The gentleman in question spoke English well. He was in the ROK army during the war attached to a marine regiment. He apparently had fond memories of his time with the corps: "Marines Number One!" The problem that brought him to the internal medicine ward was an infected bullet wound. The circumstances that resulted in his admission to our hospital were related to me by the attending physician. I will call the Korean Mr. Moon. It seems Mr. Moon was having an affair with a Korean Major's wife. While the Major was up at the 38th parallel, Mama-san was engaged in some extra-curricular activity with the aforesaid gentleman. The Major unexpectedly showed up while Mr. Moon was fully engaged in oriental coitus with the officer's wife. Being a cuckolded husband he unlimbered his .45 automatic and shot the offender about three inches above his naval The round should have gone all the way through but it didn't. The wound became infected and Mr. Moon was paying dearly for his indiscretion with a seemingly incurable staph infection. White pus drained out of a tube in his abdomen. I was incapable of providing moral or physical support over six weeks of pain. I really felt sorry for the poor man. This constituted my language practicum on Korean profanity. My vocabulary expanded exponentially. Merriam Webster could not keep up with Korean profanity. They got the jump on Westerners by about a thousand years. Even Samuel Johnson would have been flummoxed with attempting a translation. Suffice to say, the gentleman finally got better. He invited me to his home and offered to supply me with female companionship. I politely declined, not wishing a dalliance with another officer's wife and experiencing similar consequences. On the day of his discharge, his wife showed up. About ten years younger than the recovered adulterer and beautiful. What possessed him? The lure of *forbidden fruit*!

Chapter 2

January 1967

Packing was quite easy with no one to bother him. Pete packed his clothing in a suitcase placed it in the back of his Volkswagen and departed. No Phi Beta Kappa key, no au revoir, Alma Mater. You flunked out stupid. No career in science, no future, and a war going on in South-East Asia. No girlfriend, no 2-S Deferment. Hello, draft board! It was such a nice place too. Northern Illinois University had a beautiful campus in those days. Woods fronted the main entrance. Altgeld Hall was a monument to the past, a limestone edifice named in honor of the Illinois Governor who pardoned the surviving Haymarket Martyrs. It was a long drive back to Chicago; time to ponder the future which looked pretty bleak. I suppose I should look for a job. I reached home and unpacked my suitcase. My mother said very little, her disappointment was palpable. Three and one-half years down the drain with nothing to show for it save an Associate Degree from the local junior college. I started to drown my troubles in drink. One evening in a booze induced stupor the phone rang. I jumped out of bed and stepped on the empty beer glass. The broken glass could not have done more damage. Arterial blood squirted out of my foot, a jet of red with each beat of my heart. Blood quickly covered the linoleum floor. Fortunately, my levis were folded over a chair. I used my belt as a tourniquet and staunched the flow. I was home alone and managed to call the fire department for aid. The ER doctor whistled when he saw the resultant damage. Only thirty stitches, the problem was I could not walk. The hospital kindly provided me with crutches so I could hobble around until it was time to remove the stitches. Then the big Chicago blizzard of January 26, 1967 dumped twenty-six inches of snow and nothing moved.   Total Paralysis! It was a week before the roads were suitable for movement.   The stitches in my foot had grown in and the knots had to be pulled though. It was fairly obvious that the draft board would come calling soon, so I had my number pushed up.

****

July 12, 1967

Fort Leonard Wood was called "Little Korea" or "Fort Lost in the Woods", an apt name for the post. It was located on the edge of the Mark Twain National Forest in Missouri. We were housed in the old WWII yellow two-story barracks. The only feature that made the place habitable was a large fan on the second floor that effectively circulated cool air after dark. There were no insomnia problems in the company. They ran us from 5:30 A.M to 7:00 P.M. Many men gained weight. I lost twenty-five pounds. At six-feet six inches I seemed to require more calories than the ordinary trainee. There is a myth that all basic training cadre are sadists. I did not experience this. One black Staff-Sergeant, Wilson by name, was always smiling. He had Bill Cosby albums in the orderly room and played them over and over again on weekends. He particularly liked: "What's a Cubit?"

The company SFC was a Puerto Rican about 5' 8" in height and powerfully built. I went to the orderly room one afternoon to ask permission to go to the base hospital for broken and bleeding blisters on my tender University softened feet. The cure was administered by a hard punch in the stomach. My foot pain was immediately relieved. The Sergeant was tough all right. He didn't telegraph the blow, but it knocked the wind out of me.

We were all given some perfunctory tests on the nomenclature of the M-14 rifle and field hygiene. I was shocked to find out that we had a number of functional illiterates in the company. This troubled me at the time and still amazes me today. These predominately poor minorities from the South were the brain child of Robert Strange McNamara. One hundred thousand of these category three draftees constituted an armed job corps. A very bad idea indeed, I would not trust these people with a loaded rifle anywhere near me. Lyndon Johnson thought McNamara was one of the smartest men he ever knew. Possibly he was, but infantrymen cannot be stupid, especially when they have a loaded weapon in their hands. The war was never mentioned ever. Probably the powers that be thought it would be bad for morale. We spent endless hours on bayonet drill that was completely useless in the jungles of Vietnam. The prevalent theory was this elaborate minuet of parry, thrust and butt stroke would make us more aggressive. "What is the spirit of the bayonet fighter?" "Kill or be killed!" arose from the throats of one-hundred and fifty bored and distinctly non-aggressive throats. I will give the Army an A+ for their efforts to whip us into good physical condition. It was common knowledge in those days that in the course of eight weeks we would walk, run and trot a distance of at least three hundred miles. I think this total was exceeded in our company.

I could not imagine how a trainee could survive basic training at Ft. Leonard Wood during the winter. Summers were bad enough; running around in cold weather would have finished me off.

The company commander was a tough Captain from Tennessee sporting the shoulder tab of a Ranger. The only time he ever showed up during the training cycle was once on the rifle range. He came equipped with a folding chair and sat directly behind me. It is not a good thing to be the tallest man in a company of over one-hundred and fifty men. The short troops became invisible. I stood out. The training regimen was not turning me into superman. I was thin to start with, but now, I was tending toward emaciated. The Army in those days was not up to precision shooting at bull's eye targets ala the Marine Corps. This was not very practical. WWII proved that most combat shooting was done at distances under 200 yards. Consequently, the so called "train fire course was developed". The M-14 rifle was zeroed on the 1,000 inch range. You had to fire a four shot clover-leaf pattern at a little over 25 yards. The rifle was then considered zeroed for 200 yards. For qualification you fired at pop up targets at unknown distances in the shape of a man's upper body. The targets were constructed of thick cardboard and "died" when hit. A micro-switch was triggered by a bullet strike or a ricochet and it dropped down, an NCO would score this a hit. The M-14 rifle was excellent. I could easily hit targets from the prone position at 300 yards. Even with prescription glasses. On record day, I fired Marksman one shot shy of Sharpshooter. I think my final round went through a previously fired hole. The target did not drop, but what did it matter? You had to qualify with the service rifle to graduate from basic training. If you failed you went back to a different company to try all over again. So after graduation we were given orders for further training. About one-third of the company remained at Leonard Wood to become Combat Engineers which pretty much involved mine clearance and road building. Two-thirds went to infantry AIT at various posts in the South; Ft. Benning and Ft. Knox seemed to get the bulk of the company. Four of us, only four were assigned to Ft. Sam Houston, Texas for Medical Corpsman training. Three of the four had passed the test for officer candidate school. The only openings were for infantry at Ft. Benning and artillery at Ft. Sill.

I had never seen a palm tree before. Ft. Sam Houston was an old cavalry post. The officer quarters looked like something out of "Gone with the Wind." The enlisted accommodations were the old WWII two-story yellow wooden barracks. What I found particularly appalling, was the latrine which had only eight toilets with no partitions. This was not the case at Leonard Wood, at least you received some privacy. The Army, some wag once said, was designed by geniuses to be run by idiots. It was obvious that every effort was designed to remove any vestige of individuality and develop "group think". You marched together, ate together, and shit together. It was also becoming increasingly apparent that strings were being pulled all over the place to get "fortunate sons" out of harm's way. The children of sheriffs, politicians, physicians, and lawyers were all in the National Guard or Enlisted Reserve. This was the era of George W. Bush and Mitt Romney entitlements. The 'war hawks' as it turned out, were too precious to risk in combat. I suppose it was always thus. In the Civil War, Theodore Roosevelt's father found a "substitute". So did Andrew Carnegie. Rich man's war, poor man's fight has echoed through the ages. The Romans had it right. You could not serve in the Senate unless you were a former Legionnaire: a real one, not the American variety. The final straw for me was encountering a St. Louis Cardinal Farm Team player who was in the National Guard. He bragged about the manager of the team jumping him over 200 applicants for the Missouri National Guard. Bragging!

I encountered one hang-dog private who looked downcast in my barrack one day. I said, "It's not all that bad."

He looked up at me and said, "My father was killed in the Korean War"

I replied, "Do you have any brothers or sisters?"

"Yes." He answered, "One half-brother and one half-sister."

"Your mother remarried then?"

"Yes," came the reply.

"Then by law you are a sole surviving son by your mother's first marriage."

"They said it did not count, because I have a half-brother and sister."

"You get up to The JAG office and get a legal opinion, this is not right."

The decision stood. He was stuck. No legal recourse. I hope he survived.

About mid-way through the training cycle we were ushered into the post theatre for an informative film entitled, "The Vietnam War: Honoring Our Commitments" or words to that effect. President Johnson appeared on the screen and began to speak. Loud boos emerged with gusto from the throats of over four hundred men! The lights came on and Johnson's speech was temporarily interrupted. Lt. Grey charged up onto the stage, his face beet red. If I see any man booing our Commander-in-Chief again, you will be in front of the Company Commander in the morning. He was not amused. Far from striking fear into our young hearts the thought of facing the Company Commander failed to frighten anyone.

Lt. Grey was a former football player. The physical equal or superior to any enlisted man in the company. Captain Lawrence was another matter. He stood about five feet six inches and must have weighed 135 pounds. His head was so small the polished helmet he wore reached the bottom of his nose. He looked like he could crawl into his steel pot with room to spare. How this character managed to graduate from OCS escaped me. His lack of command presence was only exceeded by his inability to pronounce simple English words correctly. "Helmet" was pronounced "hermit." "Bus" was pronounced "buff." He did not want us to succeed in medic training. We were told to "secede" as the Confederacy did from the Union. Many of these malapropisms were lost on the troops but I did not miss them. Jesus, I thought, this is what is running the operation? If the officers needed remediation, the enlisted men were losers. We were given training in placement of a trach tube. A low tracheotomy was made by cutting into the "teachea." The SFC in charge said, "You introduce this here "cannula" into this here "obturator" into that there incision." The tortured English continued day after day. A rabid dog became a "rabied" dog. A liter metric liquid measurement became a "litter" as in kitty litter. By about the fifth week of this assault on the King's English, I began to tune out.

One man saved the day, Staff Sgt. Diaz . This gentleman proudly sported a Purple Heart with Oak Leaf Cluster, a Bronze Star with Oak Leaf Cluster and the Combat Medic's Badge. He served with popular forces in Vietnam known as "Ruff Puffs" and also served in Korea. He had performed amputations in the field and was generally considered one of the best field medics around. He was also a bit of a rake. His favorite experiences consisted of R&R stories in Bankok, Thailand or "Bang Clap" as it was known in those days and in Hong Kong. "Gentlemen" (he always prefaced his comments with this remark), "When I went to Hong Kong for R&R, the people I arrived with spent all their money on Tape Decks and Cameras. I spent all my money on Nookie!" "I had two bare-ass waitresses giving me whiskey and noodles all day long." Some of his advice was very valuable. "Gentlemen, the greatest killer on the battlefield is shock and blood loss. Morphine saves lives. The blood expanders you are issued will also help maintain pressure." Diaz's lectures were always good. Always spiced with his ribald stories, of which he never seemed to run out.

Before we graduated from Ft. Sam, we had to qualify with the newly minted M-16 rifle. A hurricane had hit the coastal plain in Texas in October 1967 and everything was sodden. Nothing dried out. It was like a proverbial Asian monsoon. Finally, after things dried out we headed for Camp Bullis for rifle qualification and Tiger Land. The M-16 rifle was quite a shock. The early models of this weapon were known as the "black rifle" or the "Mattel reject" because it simply did not work. They all jammed after every three or four rounds. I was incapable of qualifying with the rifle due to the constant jamming. The senior enlisted people and the range officers made no comments pro or con. I passed. But the sinking feeling in my abdomen told me that if this happened in combat you were dead. The failure of the M-16 rifle in Vietnam was blamed on GI's too lazy to clean the weapon. The fault was with the design, and still is. The rifles we used at Camp Bullis had been cleaned by us the night before qualification. A forward assist knob was later installed at the direction of the army chief of staff. If a rifle jams you clear the weapon by ejecting the faulty round and, therefore, not pushing it further into the chamber.

Tiger Land was an experience. Before it was over, I was ambushed and killed twice. By the second day, it was becoming increasing clear that Vietnam was a very dangerous place. The make believe Vietnamese village we walked through was sown with invisible death. Landmines, Punji stick pits with sharpened bamboo stalks and mortar shells detonated by near invisible mono-filament. A nice touch was what looked to me like a bear trap. It was an actual tiger trap removed from a field in Nam, rusty, but still functional. We just about cleared the village when we came under machine gun fire. Fortunately, they were 'friendlies' firing blanks. About this time, a private behind me vomited. Tiger Land most definitely had an effect on the company. This pretty much completed the training cycle in San Antonio. Orders for Vietnam came down in dribs and drabs for a few days. I guess they were testing us to see how many would get upset. On the fourth day, the hammer fell. About five men were assigned to MFSS (medical field surgical school). This extended program turned medics into surgical nurses. No second lieutenant bar, but a cushy job in some hospital. Like most of the company, I looked forward to terminal leave. It was the chance to spend Thanksgiving 1967 at home. A few men, mostly married, applied for airborne training. This did not translate to a desire to join the "elite"; just an excuse to spend another six weeks with their wives. The bulk of the company was to report to Travis Air Force base for overseas deployment to RVN. I never saw a field order typed Vietnam, it was always RVN. It could have stood for recreational vehicle for all we knew. The weekend before we departed for home was open. Most of the company headed for the flesh pots south of the border. I went to the library and decided to read up on my future destination. I happened to stumble upon the works of Bernard Fall, the chronicler of the French Indo-China war of 1945-54. At the end of the Second World War, the old colonial empires of the late 19th and early 20th centuries began to crumble. The British left India in 1947. The Belgians left the Congo. The Dutch left the East Indies. France would not let go and tried to reestablish a colonial presence in Indo-China. The Vietnamese had witnessed and experienced the Japanese occupation and realized Orientals could win. They were not about to surrender to any other nation again. The war lasted nine years, largely paid for by the United States. Vietnam was partitioned along the 17th parallel and the south became independent under a Roman Catholic Mandarin who sat out the 1950's in the home of Francis Cardinal Spellman in New York. The elections that were to be held in 1956 to determine if the southerners would vote to rejoin the Communist north were never held. The Eisenhower administration and John Foster Dulles, a staunch anti-communist, would not permit it. Had the French left Indo-China with the grace of the British in India, there would have been no French Indo-China War or the subsequent Vietnam War. I spent the better part of Saturday and Sunday absorbed in Mr. Fall's two seminal books: <u>Street Without Joy</u> and <u>Hell In A Very Small Place</u>. Bernard Fall, who accompanied Mary McCarthy to South Vietnam in 1967, was killed while on patrol with the U.S Marines.

My morale, at this point, had reached its nadir and all my reading up on the subject did not improve it. Messianic hatred of Communism had brought us to this place in time. George Kennan predicted that Communism would self-destruct. It was an economic system that simply did not work. His predictions came to pass in 1989. Nevertheless, the collapse of Communism was still far in the future, and barring some sort of miracle, would continue for us.

When I arrived home on Thanksgiving Eve 1967, my Mother greeted me at the front door and began to cry. I had lost twenty-five pounds in four months. She did not look very well and I immediately asked her how long it had been since she had seen a physician. As it turned out, it was a number of months. I decided it might be a good idea if we consulted the family doctor. Three days later we learned that her blood pressure was alarming high. He prescribed medication to lower it. Before we departed I requested that he write a statement attesting to the fact she was in frail condition. My mother had undergone gall bladder surgery in 1965 and had contracted a life threatening post-operative infection. It had settled in her ear and salivary glands. Her inner ear was permanently damaged and her face was partially paralyzed. I did not want to miss Christmas so I decided to send a telegram to the Pentagon requesting emergency leave. Several days before my terminal leave expired on December 17th I received a letter that the leave extension was approved. I could not believe it! Two additional weeks! I was told to report to Ft. Sheridan, Illinois on December 18th to await further orders. The casual company at the post consisted of people like me who had family problems. We slept in the barracks Monday through Friday and participated in work details every day. I dug a ditch along with several others to replace a ruptured water pipe in an administration building. We shoveled snow, packed boxes in a warehouse and, on one memorable day, replaced carpeting in a Colonel's living room. On weekends we were allowed to go home. Mom's condition seemed to improve with the knowledge that her only son was out of harm's way, at least temporarily. Weeks passed, we ushered in New Year 1968 off post. The casuals were allowed to go to the neighboring village of Highland Park to celebrate. Two weeks passed and still my emergency leave was in effect. I began to think that they had forgotten about me. By the middle of January I was becoming concerned. My status in limbo was beginning to bother me. I wanted a change of scenery. About the third week in January I went to the Company Commander and asked about my orders. He said he would look into it. The suspicion was correct, they had forgotten about me. I finally received a paper to report to Oakland Army terminal on or about February 3, 1968 for overseas movement to Vietnam. I cannot say I was happy, but the extra time stateside was deeply appreciated. My half-sister promised to look in on Mom even though she had three young children to care for.

Chapter 3

I thought about the young lady in the red dress and wanted to meet her again, to thank her for the gift she bestowed on me. I went back to the showboat club and was unable to find her. The "business girls" worked various clubs so they would seem "fresh" to the gullible GI's who frequented them. After about a week she turned up, she did not seem to recognize me at first. I was very forgettable except for my extreme height. We got back to her hooch and she began to remove her clothing. I stopped her. "I am hungry," I said. She gave me a look that would frighten a herpetologist, and said, "You go get some." I replied, "I am too tired. You get some!" Time is money, as they say and this lady did not want to waste it on me. Wishing to avoid a confrontation she smiled weakly and said, "I go. You wait here." I looked around her sparse room searching for a blunt object to use in case she returned with some men to eject me. Violence against soldiers was rare in Korea. The South-Koreans genuinely hated their northern cousins and held Americans in high regard. To my surprise she returned in ten minutes with two bowls of steaming noodles and shrimp. She offered me a bowl, but I took the one she was holding for herself. She seemed to instantly understand the gesture and smiled faintly. I did not want to wind up unconscious or dead outside of town. We talked. She spoke passable English. I asked her why she was a bar girl. She looked at me with genuine amazement and said, "Easy money." Apparently she was the daughter of a poor rural farmer, and did not want to spend her adult life ankle deep in mud. Without an education she had no chance to better herself, and simply ran away from home. I finished my noodles and gave her one hundred won. She seemed genuinely shocked that I did not want sex. I left.

Weeks passed. Still on the extra duty roster I spent many nights sleeping on a mattress in the emergency room. One morning, a young soldier was wheeled into the hospital bleeding from his foot. His boot was still on. It seems this GI was the proud Papa of a new baby girl. He applied for emergency leave which was denied. Resorting to what he conceived of as a plan to get back to the states he went to the arms room and asked to clean his rifle. Requests like this were commonly granted due to the fact Americans were getting killed along the DMZ in what later became known as the "Second Korean War." The young man managed to secure a round of ammunition and in the presence of the unfortunate clerk, chambered the cartridge and shot himself in the foot. The bullet penetrated the boot, the foot and ricocheted off the cement floor, striking the clerk in the abdomen. The proud father suffered a superficial wound. The bullet didn't even break the metatarsal. The clerk, however, was seriously injured. Lead fragments and portions of copper jacket entered his abdomen and penetrated his liver. The general surgeon entered the O.R looking like an avenging angel. Two other surgeons were fighting to save the "Arms Room" clerk's life. The doctor shouted at the offending G.I., "If the soldier in the next room dies, I am personally going to see you spend the next twenty years in jail. Stupid son-of-a-bitch!" At this point the blubbering idiot probably wished he could change places with the poor fellow in the neighboring O.R. I had to hold the soldier's foot up in the air to slow the bleeding. Iodoform gauze was pulled through the wound and it was easily stitched up. I believe the gut-shot clerk survived. I cannot remember. Like so many others, out of sight, out of mind. In the medical corps you cannot dwell on the fate of your patients.

About this time I was introduced to Kim Soon Kang, a Korean nurse that spoke excellent English. Like so many others, she had lost both her parents in the War. Her mother had died of starvation and her father simply disappeared. She was raised by Canadian Methodist missionaries. She had the most beautiful cursive writing that was unusual for an Asian. Quiet and efficient, we worked together for months. Somehow, I do not remember why, we wound up working the night shift together. One afternoon, I came on duty and she was unusually withdrawn. I asked, "What is the matter Mrs. Kim?" She looked at me and sighed. "My husband is staying out late and is eating dog again." For the uninitiated, eating dog was associated with male virility. Asians believe ground rhinoceros horn, tiger gall bladders, and dog meat are aphrodisiacs. Mrs. Kim believed her husband was playing the field. Why she confided in me, I will never know. At the time she already had a child and was afraid her husband would leave her. Many of the Korean women who worked for the Army would come to work on Monday mornings battered and bruised. Their husbands routinely beat them, especially on weekends. To say that women were an underclass would be an understatement. Third term abortions were not uncommon in Korea. Often, when in labor, the unwanted child would have its head pierced by a pointed steel rod and killed. Had it not been for my assignment in the 642 hospital, I would have been unaware of these procedures. If a child was born with a physical deformity of any kind, it was simply wrapped in a blanket and taken "to the mountain", a euphemism for death by exposure. While such practices were shocking to those of us schooled in western mores, the Koreans were not constrained by Judeo-Christian ethics. It was simply a fact of life. There were no provisions at that time for care of the infirm. Life was difficult enough for the healthy. The elderly were treated much better and generally honored by their children and the community. After I left the army we corresponded for years until her untimely death from breast cancer in the late 1970's.

Like Phillip Carey pursuing Mildred in <u>Of Human Bondage</u>, I found myself back in the environs of the Showboat club looking for my noodle provider. She approached me and asked, "You still hungry?" Apparently there were no hard feelings. I will call her "Yobo" Korean for honey. Yobo was intelligent, she had her life all planned. It turned out that her sister was living in a middle-class section of Seoul. I met the sister who had a small child. She was mortified that a member of her family was pandering to the sexual needs of common soldiers.

Prostitutes, especially those that serviced Americans, were considered "un-people". They had no social status and no legal protections. Many of the girls fell in love with GIs and there were more than a few marriages. Those GIs that left the country at the end of their tours and abandoned their girlfriends often left them heart-broken. Suicide was not infrequently a preferred option. Yobo was hardened to conditions and told me she was contemptuous of her clients and the girls that allowed themselves to fall in love. Why she confided in me, was a mystery. I was tall, gangling and homely by Hollywood standards. Yet, she was full of surprises. One evening I came upon her knitting me a pair of socks. She smiled and said, "For You." I knew I was costing her time and money. The need for communication among people is very strong and beneath the cynicism and coldness there was, still, a human being. I did not want the relationship to continue and hated myself for ever getting involved. I stopped going to the village, and cut off contact with her after several weeks. Less than a week later, a sergeant approached me with a message. Yobo was not eating and refused to leave her room. She wanted to see me. I did not want to see her. I was angry at myself for getting involved with a bar girl. Yobo would not give up. More messages. I finally decided to see her and break it off in person. As soon as the neighboring Koreans saw me they evidenced concern. "She sick. No eat. Stay home." Yobo was curled up in her bed and looked distraught. "Why you hurt me?" This was no act. She looked sick, and had lost weight. I could not understand it. One moment she was a hardened whore, the next she would not eat in my absence. My own stupidity had gotten me into the proverbial Cul-de-sac. I remained until evening and departed.

Tom Grimaldi had a steady girlfriend in the ville'. He made considerably more money than me. I was still a private and would remain one until I returned to the States. A high profile enlisted man in the army is poison. "Break it off ", he advised me. You don't want to marry her do you?" No, that was not an option.

The new company commander summoned us to the base theatre and introduced himself.

"Good morning men I am Captain Sideburns. My door is always open if you have some problem. There is a matter I want to discuss with you, I have seen better hair styles in Haight-Ashbury. At 0-800 tomorrow we will have a company formation in front of the hospital and I will personally inspect each of you for hair length." This character had never been within five miles of Haight-Ashbury but the war on hair had begun! Sure enough at 0-800 we assembled in front of the hospital and the company commander showed up with the first sergeant in tow carrying a clip board. The miscreants that exhibited untidiness in their personal coiffure were ordered to get a haircut within 48 hours or suffer the consequences! There were two barber shops on base. One was within the confines of the hospital with a male barber. The other was at the opposite side of the compound and run by women. The hospital shop had a queue of troops that stretched out into the corridor, at least an hour wait. I trudged over to the other side of the base to the practically empty female shop. Getting a hair cut from a Korean barber is as close to a sexual experience as you will get on this planet. When it comes time to trim the back of your head logic dictates an approach from the rear. Not on your life! They leaned directly over you and attempted the cutting from your immediate front. This necessitated a pair of breasts pushed hard into your face. The need for air was overcome by shock. I am no expert on mammography but these middle-age mama-sans seemed to be considerably better endowed than the young girls in the village. After the show was over I had to pay up. They charged more! The little capitalists knew what they were doing. I never returned.

Captain Sideburns could not be mollified, nor could the Army. No matter how much we trimmed, combed and pomaded it was never good enough. I am not surprised that forty years later all the hair was gone. Our heroes now paraded down Main Street as clean as newly laid eggs. It never occurred to the colonels in the 'five sided puzzle palace' in Washington that the U.S. Army fought the most bitter and costly battles in history from 1861 to 1865. The opposing armies had hair that stretched to their shoulders and beards that approached their navels. Chalk it up to discipline. If the officers wanted to keep us angry they succeeded. About this time I got wind of a plot to do away with the company Sergeant Major. I was never privy to the plot because I was not on good terms with most of the enlisted men in the company. I think they resented my vocabulary. When I spoke, I often unconsciously used words they did not understand. It was not intentional, just a consequence of writing term papers in college. Money was passed from hand to hand and collected to pay off a "slicky boy" to do the deed. Somehow the company commander got wind of the nascent plot and sparks began to fly. Captain Sideburns temporarily gave up the fight against our crowning glory, and summoned us to the Post Theatre. Sideburns knew his career was on the line and read us the riot act, or rather the articles of war. Even in the Army the word "mutiny" is used. This would seem more appropriate if applied to Captain Bligh but is apparently universal. Mutiny is punishable by death. Even to conspire to make a mutiny is a serious crime. Apparently this short circuited the plot. The Sergeant Major did not seem such a bad fellow. He was simply doing his job. Harassment of the troops was part of that job. In an army of unwilling conscripts it had to be thus. What the fall-out from this incident was I never knew. I really wasn't interested in the Sergeant Major's fate or Capt. Sideburns either.

Several weeks later, we were again told to report to the Post Theatre at a given hour. Was the plot against the Sgt. Major on again? The company commander was nowhere to be seen. The hospital commander strode up to the stage followed by the urologist. LTC Odell looked distinctly uncomfortable. He cleared his throat and began, "Men, the venereal disease rate in Inchon is approaching epidemic proportions. All passes and leaves will be cancelled until further notice. We have some slides we would like to show you." The house lights were lowered and in living color we viewed an array of infected penises with every conceivable disease evolution could devise in a million years: Yellow pus, red blood, venereal warts. The photos were suitable for a Baptist revival meeting. Evil was abroad in the land. Every generation that goes to war is viewed as the finest. We have the best trained, best educated, troops in the world. They are killer priests dedicated to the preservation of FREEDOM! What is never discussed is the plain fact that the young men have genitals and like to use them.

If you ever happen to visit Gettysburg Military Park you can view a surgeon's medical instruments in a green velvet lined box. All the instruments are neatly arrayed: knives, probes, tourniquets, etc. You will also notice depressions in the green velvet that look like they would accommodate soda straws curved at each end. The instruments are missing. They are called "sounds" or "dilators" used to treat gonorrhea. Antibiotics were not widely used until the 1940's. The treatment in the Civil War was painful. A hollow "sound" was introduced into the urethra and silver nitrate was poured in. This killed the diplo-cocci bacteria but also scarred the urethra. At regular intervals the urethra had to be dilated by the solid "sounds" to keep it open. Over 200,000 union troops became infected during the Civil War. At one time, there were over 400 brothels in Washington D.C. The men called them "Headquarters" U.S. Army. In WWII, General Claire Lee Chenault allowed importation of Indian women to Kunming, China to keep the Flying Tigers happy. The VD rate sky rocketed and the acerbic theatre commander, "Vinegar Joe" Stilwell, put an end to it. In Liege, Belgium in 1944, there were large brothels that serviced thousands of soldiers A "pro-kit packet" was issued to the troops to keep down infection rates. The inability of the Army to deal with this problem in Vietnam and Korea was a denial of reality.

The next day a phalanx of doctors descended on Bupyong with tongue depressors to do vaginal smears. Yobo was one of the supervisors, a foreman so to speak. The results were not encouraging.

Rumors began to circulate that a lot of ROK soldiers were being killed along the eastern portion of the DMZ. Years later I found out that the North Koreans were landing agents by submarine along the east coast to start a popular uprising among the farmers. We were all aware that the crew of the Pueblo was in North Korean custody since Jan 23, 1968, but had scant knowledge of the appearance of armed North Korean Special Forces shooting it out with the ROK army. Later, I learned that 299 ROK soldiers were killed between 1966-69 with over 500 wounded. Virtually no Americans are aware that these events transpired. Vietnam is a fading memory. The first Gulf War forgotten. The firefights along the DMZ were seldom discussed, but the ville wars were ongoing.

****

There was strict segregation in Sinchon when it came to business with black soldiers. The double-eagle club was for black GI's only. It was dangerous for minorities to enter white only bars and vice versa. Some of the girls preferred African-Americans or "Gum dingies." Many preferred white only clients. I asked Yobo about it she said, Blacks too "taksan" (big in other words). Painful intercourse was frowned upon. The ville' girls were tough. I saw a "cat" fight outside a club one night. One business girl knocked down another and proceeded to kick her in the head. All of the ladies were required to carry V.D. cards that supposedly insured they were disease free. The ones that had active disease lost their cards and were relegated to BJ alley. These females gave blow jobs for 250 won. They had few clients.

A quiet new addition to the 642 hospital had his own solution to the problem of Sinchon. This new PFC fresh from the states found out about the place and filled out a formal requisition for ten hand grenades. He wanted to blow up the clubs! The Army form was filled out correctly and placed by the PFC in the "In" box in the orderly room. He was quite serious and very crazy. Needless to say, he didn't get the requested items. His disappearance caused barely a ripple. Where they sent him:

remained a mystery.

Some of you may wonder why I write of these incidents so many years after they occurred. The answer is simple. Now that I am an old man, I dusted off my notes of long ago and tried to come to grips with the twenty-four year old that was once me. I have some difficulty understanding my thinking or lack thereof. At bottom it had to do with boredom and loneliness. Yobo's hootch was a refuge and an oasis. I could read, listen to records, sleep and generally get away from it all. The fact that I did not have to pay for anything was both lucky and burdensome. I was interfering with business and mooching off a whore. One night after curfew, Yobo decided I should leave immediately. I could not leave after 11:00 P.M as I would be caught and detained either by the national police or the 728 military police. She started yelling and screaming, "Ka, Go compound!" I grabbed her by the shoulders and shook her and told her to be quiet. She continued, "Get out, get out!" I slapped her hard. "Ka, go compound" I slapped her hard again. She stopped yelling and fell into bed. I figured this was it. She found someone else and couldn't be bothered with me. I lay down on the floor and fell asleep. At first light, I got dressed and quietly left. I had negotiated about fifty yards and Yobo was running after me yelling, "Don't go, you stay! I sorry!" Maybe she was on drugs or crazy or both. This whole situation was spinning out of control. I was afraid she would injure herself or me.

I sought the counsel of Tom Grimaldi. He shook his head and said, "Get out before something really bad happens." I had to agree. Like a moth attracted to a flame it was difficult to break it off. Yobo was cute and smart. If she was crazy; what of it? So was I. Since the enlisted men I served with were mostly high school drop-outs and not very interesting, where could I turn? It seemed my future was in doubt and my past was forever gone.

One night in the emergency room, a young black man walked into the hospital holding his right hand. A blood trail was visible behind him like the pebbles in a Hansel and Gretel story. I asked him to open his hand. I immediately felt the urge to throw up. The young man had gotten into some sort of fracas with another GI. Words were exchanged. A knife was pulled and the attacker's blade was grabbed by the intended victim. His attempts to disarm his assailant must have been successful, no other wounds were visible. He paid dearly for his self-defense. The emergency room clerk awakened the sleeping plastic surgeon who arrived on the scene in a semi-awake condition. The sight that greeted him snapped him to wakefulness. He appeared to turn green. The wounded GI was attended to but was gone within three days. Reconstruction surgeries necessary were beyond the capabilities of our Evac hospital. Many years later my wife and I went to the local theatre to see the film "Rob Roy." At one point in the movie, Liam Neeson grabs the sword blade of the actor, Tim Roth, who is about to kill him. I got up and left the theatre. The image proved to be too powerful.

Some ex-GIs talk about their luck: I was lucky to survive; Joe got hit and I came through. My luck was about nil. Every time something happened I seemed to be at or near the problem. Mrs. Kim Soon Kang and yours truly were on duty second shift on Internal Meds. We were also covering the hepatitis ward. Suddenly, I heard a loud bang and the crash of glass in the adjoining ward. I raced over to see what was going on. I knew about the prisoner with hepatitis, but I did not know why he was hand-cuffed to his bed. Apparently he had gotten jaundice and blamed it on his girl friend. He beat her up and stabbed her. The MP on the ward looked worried and said he had to go to the bathroom. He handed his .45 automatic to me and left. That was the last I ever saw of him. Some of the other patients were out of bed and giving me dirty looks. Suddenly, the lights went out! Someone had gotten behind me and switched them off. I had no intention of shooting anyone so I backed out of the ward and went to the nurse's station in the adjoining ward. I got on the phone and called the O.D. in the receiving room. "Lieutenant we have a problem on C-12. The patients are out of their beds. They have broken the television and switched off the lights. The little

Hawaiian MP ran away and gave me his pistol."

"I'll be right there, Private." The O.D. arrived on the scene and entered the ward. By this time several pillows had been ripped open and the patients were walking around in the vicinity of the broken glass. The lieutenant disappeared. Within five minutes a contingent of the 728 M.P. Company appeared with shotguns and side arms.

The company First Sergeant arrived and immediately saw the .45 Colt in my hand. "What are you doing with that pistol private? Do you realize you are not authorized to carry a weapon in the hospital? This is a court-martial offense!" I explained that the MP had taken off to go to the bathroom and never returned. He took the weapon and departed. By this time additional medics had arrived. We cleaned up the broken glass and destroyed television and got the patients back to bed. The MPs remained for the rest of the night. Nothing was said regarding the incident. I was never asked about it. The commander wanted the incident expunged from the hospital log. It would not look good on the record and might spoil the possibility for a promotion down the line. I am not surprised the My Lai massacre was suppressed for a year. If it wasn't for the photographs taken at the time no one would have ever known.

A word about our Non-Commissioned Officers (NCOs) referred to as "No Chance on the Outside" by the draftees. There was another category I personally invented: Non-Commissioned Alcoholics. The drinking that went on was mind boggling. After hours, many, if not most of our contingent of leaders, were half in the bag. The worst example was the Sgt. who was supposedly in charge of the X-ray room. I would come on duty and he was sitting behind his desk sleeping. A little Italian Buck Sergeant ran the whole operation. Sgt. Arbor Vitae was out of it most of the time. Nothing was done, ever. The logic being a warm body in any condition was better than an absent one. Vietnam was the priority, no doubt about it. Sgt. Helborn, the gentle Alabamian, thought I was funny. He called me "Old Schmoo". He drank his Old Overholt rye straight. No water, no ice, eight ounces at a time, like soda pop. One memorable day the old Sergeants decided to show us how to hike. It was on a Saturday morning, as I recall. All "off duty" personnel met outside the hospital entrance and the senior NCOs led the way. Off we went at a brisk pace. After the first mile or two, the speed began to slow perceptibly. At mile three, our leadership began to turn red. By mile five, they began to drop out. The short-timers such as myself hadn't even broken a sweat. We were prepared to march as far as Pyongyang, if necessary, to embarrass these characters. Finally, we were all alone. No more sergeants. They had all crapped out. Some wag ordered a "halt" and "about face" We marched back to the base in triumph. Did these old codgers actually think they could keep up with a group of twenty-year olds? One of the afore mentioned sergeants was so undermined by the experience, he put in orders for Vietnam. He was gone in a week. His name was never mentioned in any context again.

It was about ten-thirty, one night, when several medics came in the barracks laughing like hell. Tears were streaming down their cheeks. It seems an inebriated enlisted man had gone down on one of the business girls. In an alcohol induced erotic haze he had bitten her hard on her labia majora. In a howl of pain and indignation she attempted to jump out of bed. The GI would have none of it. He wanted to complete the act. Apparently her screams had attracted several Korean men who always seemed to hover around the 'boom-boom' houses. The GI wound up in the ER bleeding from the nose and mouth. The locals were in hot pursuit. This was an insult to Korean womanhood! Besides she could no longer work. Her equipment would not be functional for some time. An apology and money was sought. It was referred as "Working women's compensation," so to speak. How this situation was resolved I never found out. Such matters were quickly buried. The GI and the young lady survived.

This is not to suggest that all officers and enlisted men were disloyal to their wives and sweet hearts. Many men were shocked and disgusted by what was going on and remained faithful. They stayed on Post, playing cards or watching "Laugh-in" or "Star Trek" on our one channel.

Morris Lowenstein, a dermatologist, invited me to his son's circumcision ceremony off base. The Doctor was a non-practicing Jew but his wife was reform and kept a Kosher home. There were no Rabbis in Korea, so the army flew in the only active duty Chaplain within two thousand miles all the way from Japan. I was struck by the beauty of the doctor's wife. I said, "I did not know there were any red-headed Jews."

Dr. Lowenstein smiled and said, "My wife's parents left Hungary in 1938, the rest of the family perished in WWII." He generously offered to invest my money in the stock market, but at seventy-one dollars a month my potential portfolio would have been miniscule. He made no secret of the fact that he thought the Vietnam War was a travesty but he seldom discussed his political views.

To do justice to this story, gentle reader, I must discuss the hardest part of my experience in the medical corps: The maimed and injured children. Fifteen years had elapsed since the end of the first Korean War, but there was still death everywhere. The earth was seeded by every type of deadly missile imaginable: unexploded grenades, mortar rounds, artillery shells and the ever-present mines. All types of them; Anti-personnel, anti-tank, you name it. They were supposed to have a life-span of about seven to ten years in the ground. Not so. My most vivid and lasting impression of this tragic situation was a beautiful four-year-old who came in minus her left leg. The Anesthesiologist was especially stricken. He said, "Poor little kid, her pelvis will never grow normally, no one will ever marry her." Another child came in minus her lower jaw and she had to be fed with a device that resembled a poultry baster. It had a rubber bulb and a stainless steel tube to introduce liquid nourishment into the esophagus. She still had a swallow reflex and could ingest liquid food. I only spent one full day on this surgery ward. Apparently, I was called in because the duty medic was incapable of enduring another day with this patient. Back on my ward we received a Korean boy who had been struck by a U.S. Army truck. It must have been a glancing blow otherwise he would have been killed. The poor kid had steel pins in his leg and was in traction. He was placed on our ward due to the fact Mrs. Kim Soon Kang our night nurse could communicate with him. I thought I would do the kid a favor one afternoon and went to the mess hall and secured an ice-cream cone. He looked appalled and made a face. I realized, then, that he probably had never seen ice cream before. Licking the cone and smiling I tried again. Still no response, try something else. We had an ample supply of orange juice in small cardboard cartons. I opened one, placed a straw inside and offered it. He grasped it reluctantly and looked in the carton. He tried a small sip and his face lit up. I said, "orange juice". He quickly emptied the contents, pointed at the empty carton and said, "Juice-o", "Juice-o". In three days the supply of orange juice was practically exhausted. I had to go to another ward to replenish the larder. Whenever I came on duty, I was greeted by a beatific smile and the word. "Juice-o"

When any soldier was on R&R, I was called as a filler or "floater." One day I was on duty in the operating room and another beautiful little child, the daughter of an American soldier and a Korean woman came in. She had auburn hair and an oriental face. Somehow she had gotten a bottle of lye and swallowed it. Her esophagus was terribly scarred and had to be dilated with a hard rubber hose. Audrey had the most sad and resigned face I ever saw on a child. I will not detail the mechanics of the dilatation. Suffice to say, it was very painful to watch and more painful to endure. This poor kid was indeed scarred for life.   After   some months of this tedium and trauma, I was getting jumpy and irritable. I decided to do something about it. Thorazine is a major muscle relaxant and anti-psychotic medication used prior to surgery. Securing an ampule, I filled a syringe and injected it into my right buttock. In less than a minute it took effect. My right leg collapsed under me, I could not stand up. Apparently the thorazine had gone directly to my sciatic nerve and paralyzed my leg. "Oh shit," I thought. "What if it doesn't
wear off? They will send me up the river forever!" I managed to

crawl into a bathroom and lift myself onto a commode. I figured my absence could be explained by a loose bowel. The minutes dragged on, no return of feeling, no possibility of locomotion. Someone entered the room and relieved themselves. Fortunately, they paid no attention to me. After about an hour feeling gradually returned to my leg. I was able to walk again, albeit haltingly. I never again experimented with any drug.

It was impossible to keep Milk of Magnesia in storage. It disappeared almost immediately. The problem was with the national agriculture. Human waste was used for fertilizer. Untreated human waste contains all sorts of nasty parasites and bacteria. Despite the best efforts of the Quartermaster Corps and locked doors, no Milk of Magnesia was ever around. I found out why. One day I came on duty and saw Nurse Pierce with an emesis basin pulling round worms out of the nose and mouth of a dying Korean. The little bastards knew their host was expiring and were abandoning the sinking ship. These nematodes were smart but they did not cooperate. They wanted out but did not want to be pulled out! They were the by-products of polluted water.

By this point in my military career, I realized the possibility of rising in the ranks was impossible. I would remain a private until I served my time. Three-hundred and ninety-seven days. I was counting the hours, days, and minutes until deliverance.

Back in the emergency room on night duty again, I was roused from my slumbers by the O.D. The redeeming part of this extra duty was both the duty physician and enlisted medic were allowed to sleep if nothing was happening. Napoleon said, "The greatest quality in a soldier is constancy in the face of hardship" Military service, he might have added, murders sleep. In Vietnam, a day of humping in the jungle was followed by a night of on-and-off vigil on guard. Wiping off my face with the back of my hand, I went down to the mess-hall barracks to see what the problem was. The scene that greeted me resembled the final reel in a Keystone cops film. The barrack was in complete disarray. The beds were overturned, the kerosene space heater had been knocked over and kerosene had been spilled on the floor. Blankets and pillows were scattered around. Hillbilly Evans was pinioned buck-naked to an inner-spring bunk being held down by four black mess men. These guys were from the inner-city and not to be trifled with. They were showing remarkable restraint given the circumstances. Evans was screaming, "Leave me alone! Get off of me! Mother-fuckers! I'll kill all of you!" The mess-men stared at me waiting for my reaction. Evans was trying to bite the men restraining him and was literally frothing at the mouth. I had never witnessed a scene like this before or since. I told him to knock off the nonsense and get a grip on himself. He looked me straight in the eye and said, "Fuck you! You four-eyed motherfucker!" With that, I raised my hand above my head and slapped him hard on the face. He immediately stopped thrashing around and looked me straight in the eye and said coldly and believably: "I am going to kill you, you Sonofabitch!" I had no reason to doubt his word. One mess-man grabbed his right arm and another on his left. He walked to the hospital, no further resistance. Now I had something else to think about: a knife in the back some dark evening.

Chapter 4

June 9, 1953

I had just returned from school. It was my final day before summer recess. Lounging in the living room watching television I heard a car stopping in front of our home. Ordinarily, this would not have caused me to move from my comfortable position on the couch. For some reason, I knew this was different. Call it a premonition. I walked over to the window and saw a police car parked directly in front of our home. This never happened, it looked like the officers were discussing something. One shook his head, the other opened the door and they walked over our lawn and climbed the stairs. The doorbell rang. By this time my mother was in the living room and answered the doorbell. The officer was very polite, "Mrs, Sirkin, I am sorry to inform you that your husband died at work about two hours ago. We have no details." My mother began to weep, and so did I. Leaving the front room, I found myself sitting on the back yard lawn, crying. The neighbor lady, Mrs. Mika, asked what was wrong. I said, "My father died today." "I am so sorry," she said. She immediately stopped hanging her washing on the clothesline and went indoors. The next few days were a blur. I remember the local Masonic Lodge showed up for the funeral and delivered the eulogy. The funeral home was small but three hundred people showed up. I never understood why. My father died a broken and penniless man. His business failed and he spent the remainder of his life paying off his debts and working three jobs. After his obligations were met, he simply dropped dead: a massive heart attack at the age of 52. My mother had to find work, quickly, to support my half-sister, my grandmother and me. I was pretty much on my own from then on. It is very difficult to grow up quickly. Age nine is too early to assume responsibility for preparing your own meals and getting dressed in the morning. Granny was already up in years and had raised her own seven children. She had been in the United States since 1904 but had never bothered to learn English. She clearly stated her lack of interest in raising the widow's son or step-daughter. From 8:00 A.M. to 6:00 P.M., my sister and I were on our own.

My escape from this grim reality was books. I loved to read and spent a great deal of time at the local library. My sister was not a reader and made fun of me for "wasting all my time reading." Even my grandmother chimed in, "He is lazy!" How many ten-year-old kids are ambitious? When I did watch television, I confined myself to the "Lone Ranger" and "Sky King". There were many variety shows in those days and everyone watched "Ed Sullivan" on weekends. Later on, "Have Gun Will Travel" was a favorite, as well as the "Twilight Zone" and I never missed an episode. I thought Rod Serling was a hero. He was a World War II vet who would not tolerate compromise with bigotry or racism. Ed Morrow was another favorite. I watched "Person To Person" after Boy Scouts on Friday evenings. My sister worked at the local movie theatre so from about 1954 to 1956 I saw every movie made in Hollywood. The local movie theatre also showed Italian movies with subtitles. This was unusual at the time. It probably had something to do with the projectionist being an Italian. I respected Roberto Rosselini. I think the Ritz theatre was the only movie house in fifty miles that showed "Open City". My uncles and aunts did not interest me at all. Two of them frequented the local golf course but, beyond that, they didn't seem to know much of anything. My younger uncle was constantly making derogatory remarks about Negroes. For example, "What do you call a Black Astronaut? Answer: Shine On Harvest Moon." I did not like or appreciate his racist jokes. My aunt, for some strange reason, disliked American Indians. I never figured that one out. The nearest Indians were two hundred miles away in Wisconsin. I was no stellar student but did well in science, English and history. I struggled with mathematics for years. My uncles never took any interest in me at all. As children and young adults during the depression, making a living was all that concerned them. Everything else was off the radar. My younger uncle watched the weekend football games and was especially interested in basketball. He had received a basketball scholarship at Marquette University but dropped out. I assumed it was academics that did him in but I never asked and he never volunteered. The Uncle that I really liked and admired lived in Pontiac, Illinois. He was gassed in WWI and suffered bouts of terrible coughing that went on for minutes at a time. I am seventy years old now and few people younger than me experienced the ravages of mustard gas coughing. It was terrible and frightening. One day in 1952 he started coughing so badly he suffered a cerebral hemorrhage and died. He was 56 years old.

Arts and letters were not very important in my family. My mother had never attended high school. She could not help me with my homework. My sister was a Candy Striper at the local hospital and entertained thoughts of becoming a nurse but dropped out of high school and got married at 18. When she moved away, there was no sadness. The social security survivor benefits that we received after my father's death kept a roof over our heads. Thanks to this government largesse and a state scholarship I became a life-long liberal and proud progressive. I graduated from high school in 1962. Not exhibiting any particular talents for anything, I worked at a paint factory for a year. This was an absolute dead end. I made up my mind and had to go to college! In 1963 I began work at the local community college where I graduated in 1965 with an Associate's Degree. I was then accepted at Northern Illinois University. I decided to major in Chemistry. The Salutatorian of our high school graduating class was in the program with me. Physical Chemistry and Calculus, however, did me in. Mandy graduated; I didn't. Years later, I met her again at our 25th High School Reunion. She told me her faculty advisor, whose name I will not mention, told her, "I hope you are never a practicing bench chemist." All Hail and farewell, she became the medical librarian at Northwestern University.

****

I floated ward to ward. Mostly, I spent my time in Internal Medicine where nothing dramatic ever happened, most of the time. I kept one eye open at night waiting for the knife under the ribs from the hillbilly. He glared at me when we passed in the halls, but never spoke to me again. One night I was called to C-7 the Psychiatric Ward where a young infantryman was having a terrible nightmare. He was dreaming about a North Korean body he was ordered to retrieve in an area around outpost Dort on the DMZ. It was late at night and there were some suspicious sounds to their immediate front. Fortunately, the auditory acuity of one of the soldiers was excellent. The nearest weapon was a Browning .50 caliber machine gun. He triggered a long burst followed by silence. In the morning a group of GIs found the body or what was left of the body. The North Korean had received the full burst in his chest. When they attempted to lift the corpse it fell apart. This was too much for one of the litter bearers. The infantryman freaked out. Several days later he was discharged from the hospital and appeared to be all right.

I have spent a good deal of time discussing the loves of the straight members of our unit. Let me turn to the gay members for a moment. These events transpired decades before don't ask don't tell propounded by Bill Clinton. The military is simply a cross-section of middle and lower middle class America. There have always been gays in the military. None other than Lawrence of Arabia was a masochist gay man who paid men to beat him. Lord Kitchner, the famous English general pictured on the WWI poster, "Your King and Country Need You", was gay. A member of George Washington's officer corps was drummed out of the continental army for diddling an enlisted man. His sword was broken over his head.

The military is a perfect place for gay men: few women and an ample supply of buddies. In the Alaskan theatre in WWII the Army was confronted with an epidemic of homosexual behavior. With no women and unlimited time to kill the soldiers began to have sex with each other. Human beings in this regard, are not much different from rats. If females are removed from a cage after a week or so the males will begin to mount each other. I encountered two individuals who were active gays. One an officer, one enlisted. I will not discuss the two nurses who were sent back to the states for their lesbian affair because it was hushed up so quickly we humble enlisted people never were privy to the circumstances. Major Dickens was a strict regular Army nurse. He seemed to enjoy throwing his weight around and would brook no back talk from the EM. The Major's ace in the hole was his ability to get you a promotion if you were amenable to having sex with him. It seemed to work. The seamstress was kept busy sewing on stripes and Spec/4 patches on the troops. I avoided this character as much as possible. Fortunately, we seldom came in contact. Sgt. Dyer was another man. He happened to have a cubicle directly next to my bunk. NCOs were assigned to each barrack one at each end to keep an eye on the lower ranking troops. They were entitled to walled-off partitions with doors that could be locked. Unfortunately virtually every sound emanating from his room could be heard by me. Sgt Dyer had an almost unlimited liquor supply which he would freely share with his "friends". I fell in with his immediate circle and found his "Bon Homme" pleasant. That is until I realized what the game was. The sounds emanating from the cubicle at night were keeping me awake. I needed rest. I asked Yobo in the village if I could sleep on the floor in her room and explained the situation. To my amazement she agreed, as long as I arrived after dark.

Sgt. Dyer was discovered in the middle of intercourse by a tough Staff Sergeant and Vietnam vet. Dyer pled with Sgt. Jones not to turn him in. It was his career; his life. Jones promised not to do anything but clearly stated his nocturnal activities had to come to a stop.

Drug use by the middle of 1968 was already a big problem in the Far East. Marijuana was freely available. The stuff was grown locally and also brought in from Vietnam by the Air Force. There were large U.S. bases in Korea and cargo aircraft flew in from Vietnam and Japan. Whether it was the enlisted men who were doing the smuggling or they colluded with the pilots I never knew. The Vietnamese weed was powerful. Even if you were a non-druggie you had to partake of the stuff or you were considered to be a "Narc" or informer. Several drags on a joint and the Vietnamese weed put you in orbit. How efficient the infantrymen in Vietnam were after partaking of this cannabis is an open question. The Vietcong were smart, if they had given it away. One of my barrack mates lived in Hawaii. His brother was involved in the drug trade and grew "Maui Wowie" on the side. It was unnecessary to ship it to the orient as abundant supplies were available locally. LSD was another, It could be shipped in a regular envelope. One day returning from the hospital I walked into the barracks and beheld an incredible scene. I group of medics were sitting on the cement floor eating pieces of what appeared to be a letter. Joe's brother was putting drops of LSD on the paper and sending it along in the form of letters. Since no one inspected the mail it created no concerns. I was motioned to join the party but declined. Needless to say there was a downside to the use of LSD and troops on bad trips soon became a major concern. One enlisted man began to tear up the latrine in the middle of the night. He broke the mirrors with his bare hands and somehow managed to break a commode. When I went to the latrine in the morning to relieve myself, it was still a bloody mess. This alerted the powers that be that drug use was rampant among the hospital staff so the drug inspections began. In the middle of the night, about two or three in the morning the lights would abruptly be turned on and we were told to open our wall and foot lockers. We were being shaken down for drugs. This further interrupted our priceless sleep. Early morning inspections were now routinely performed. Enlisted men are not stupid, the drugs were now stored in toothpaste tubes. The sergeants never checked them.

The lengths that the senior enlisted men went to curry favor with the officers was something to behold. It was so embarrassing. They shuffled, they cooed: "Yes Sir," or "Yes Ma'am," and "Oh! You are so right, Sir!" Most of the senior sergeants were SFCs who lusted after that third rocker like a gourmet drooling over a plate of oysters at the Ritz. Only about 5% of officers ever rise above full bird colonel. Years later when I was a high school teacher, I asked the guidance counselor, who was a LTC in the Air Force reserve, how one obtained a Silver Star. He had the rank of Brigadier General. He immediately said, "You have to know a politician!" He might have also added you must be a born-again Christian. How fundamentalism has gained such power in the military is beyond my comprehension. George Washington on his deathbed was asked if he wanted a clergyman to attend him, he answered in the negative. Our founding fathers were agnostics. Thomas Jefferson doubted the divinity of Jesus Christ. The military has always been conservative but the recent turn to fundamental Christianity puzzles me. Conservatives seemingly have no sense of irony. They cannot deal with dichotomy. The great generals of the past had no difficulty with challenging questions. Read the memoirs of Sherman, Grant, Ridgeway. These were intellectually gifted men. They had vision. The current crop of Generals suffers by comparison.

The situation on the DMZ was not good in mid 1968. I found out many years later that Agent Orange was being used. . It was not being sprayed from aircraft as in Vietnam rather from the back of trucks. Many of the men of the 2nd and 7th infantry divisions who patrolled along the border are now dead; Non-Hodgkin's lymphoma was the cause in many instances.

President Reagan's Secretary of the Treasury Donald Regan stated at the height of the Iran-Contra scandal, "We have been snookered by a bunch of rug merchants." The same might be said of the Korean 'sleight of hand' artists. In a poor country one might expect theft of one sort or another. The Koreans lifted everything. Instruments were missing from the O.R. retractors. Scalpels, hemostats, you name it. It was a mystery. The hospital commander got the bright idea to start searching the Korean employees that worked in the O.R. Mr. Ahn was clipping the purloined instruments on the inside of his coat, and walking out the front gate as casually as you please. He was arrested and detained for one day. No charges were filed. A politically well-connected individual, he walked. In the O.R. one night, the bars that blocked the windows in a suite were pried apart with an automobile jack; two valuable cystoscopes were stolen. At this point guards were posted at night to prevent further thefts. Up north, just south of the Imjin River, the axle of a two and one-half ton truck was stolen in the middle of the night with two sentries standing less than 100 feet away. These equipment thefts accomplished in the dead of night under the very noses of American guards would have tested the skills of Houdini.

Toward the end of June, a new physician appeared at the 642. His crisp green fatigues betrayed his newness to the Army. A Yale graduate, he was a handsome fellow. When we met, he glared at me with a look that would have turned Lot's wife into a pillar of salt. It was obvious he hated the Army and hated Korea. Apparently his promising state side career had ended before it began. Having just completed his residency, Uncle Sam had come calling in the person of General Hershey chief of selective service. In a year of shocks to my nervous system, what transpired in the next two weeks left me numb. One day, Dr. Brahman was due to show up on my ward. He was to go on duty second shift. The floor nurse got on the phone to try to find out where he was. Minutes passed, still a no show. The phone rang and the O.D. said his whereabouts were unknown. Several days passed, as the story unfolded, two physicians went down to the village and made some polite inquiries through a Korean interpreter as to the whereabouts of the missing Captain. He was found in bed with a Korean bar girl. This was very unusual. Normally those physicians that purchased the services of the girls brought them to their own rooms. Capt. Brahman was so new to the hospital that he was unfamiliar with the standard protocol. Of course he was AWOL. He apparently did not want to leave. The doctors finally persuaded him to depart the fair damsel and return to base. He was confined to quarters and was secretly spirited out of the country. The man had completely lost it in less than a month. I believe he was either sent to the large field hospital located at

Camp Zama, Japan or sent stateside. I guarantee an enlisted man would not have gotten away with such action. I almost felt sorry for the poor bastard. I hope he had a good life under more tolerable living conditions.

The late great British anthropologist Ashley-Montagu once said, "Man is the only bi-pedal rectilinear mammal capable of being produced in large quantities by unskilled labor who enjoy their work." The answer to this perpetual search for connubial companionship is in the nature of man. Newborn humans are virtually helpless for at least five or more years after they are born, in modern America this period now extends to twenty-one years or longer. How do you keep Papa around long enough to provide provender and security for the newborn and Mama? Appeal to his humanity? Send in enough box tops? Pray? No the trick nature has provided to keep daddy close to the hearth or camp fire is sex. Man unlike most mammals requires it on a daily or at least weekly basis. We are no nobler than any beast of the field and as WWII proved, often far worse. Money may make the world go round but sex provides the lubrication.

In the summer of 1968, Dr. Stanfield applied for permission to go to Vietnam. He felt his skills as a vascular surgeon could better be utilized in a combat zone. This brilliant surgeon and very dedicated man was the finest example of a true human being I have ever met. I am sure he saved many lives. Nobility was not confined to officers. One day I passed the emergency room and heard a very muted groan. I decided to investigate. Four enlisted men were seated or standing in an ante-room. Somehow they had triggered a land mine. Apparently they were on the DMZ, gathering wood to burn for either cooking or warmth. Climbing the side of a hill bang the mine went off. I never knew for sure but I believe it was a left over from the war. Had it been newer a leg or two would have been lost. It was only a partial detonation as I later learned. Nevertheless, it was powerful enough to blast the utility uniform trousers completely off two of the men. Both legs of one of the soldiers were burned and blackened by the blast. Vegetation and pebbles were embedded in the legs of two. They uttered virtually no sound. I knew all four of them were in pain and shock but the pain was borne with stoicism. I got a lump in my throat, at that moment I realized that my decision to enter the Army was correct. I was glad to be there, and very proud of these brave men whose silence spoke volumes. I got out of the way to make room for the Doctor and two nurses. There is nothing more difficult than duty in the infantry in war time. Ernie Pyle wrote about it in WWII. Other branches are difficult, but living, sleeping, and dying in direct contact with the earth exceeded all other forms of discomfort.

More "profiles" were arriving from Vietnam these men were in condition to do limited duty, but were unfit for a war zone. Sgt. Floyd Smith was a unique example of the dangers of duty in Nam. He was in charge of a mess hall in one of the larger base camps in country. There were numerous Vietnamese contract workers laboring for their allies. These indigenous laborers had to pass rigid scrutiny in order to insure their loyalty. I asked Sgt. Smith why he was holding his head in apparent pain. He said, "I got hit!" I could detect no scarring on his cranium or any sign of trauma. Perusal of his chart showed he had suffered a severe concussion.

I asked him, "What happened?"

He replied, "The Vietnamese mess man blew up the kitchen".

"What hit you?" I inquired.

"A potato."

"What? I answered with incredulity.

"He placed the explosive in the potato masher. Fortunately the stainless steel pot missed me." This summed up the Vietnam War for me. None of our allies could be trusted. Another enlisted man told me of an incident that happened at an air base in the central highlands. Two Vietnamese showed up in business suits with a surveyor's transit and proper credentials. They set up their instruments and proceeded to survey the entire base. Two days later the airfield was mortared with considerable damage to aircraft and buildings. The Vietnamese surveyors turned out to be communist agents who somehow secured documents allowing them to enter an American base. This never happened again, as far as I knew. Some weeks later another returnee from the war zone was admitted to our ward. He was married to a Korean woman and had come directly to Seoul from Saigon. I asked him what impressed him most about his one year in country. "The corruption," was his frank reply.

A story surfaced about mid-June that a star light telescopic sight had been stolen in a village close to the Imjin River up north. The first generation night vision telescope was about the size of a roll of kitchen towels. It delivered a green grainy image of the surrounding countryside. It was an imperfect guardian of the night, but it allowed the Americans a significant advantage. It could be hand held or mounted on a rifle. In any event one was stolen. The battalion commander in the unit closest to the village bordering the American base gave the mayor 24 hours to get the scope and return it or the village would be bull dozed. According to reports it was back in 4 hours. This penchant for stealing anything that was not nailed down, and frequently material that was nailed down extended to Vietnam. The White horse division of the ROK army was sent to Vietnam as an exchange for the two under strength American divisions in Korea. The Vietnamese hated the Koreans more than the Americans. The swag stolen by the ROK army in Nam was loaded into ocean going ships and sent to Inchon. The bodies of the dead ROK army soldiers never returned, their ashes did. Cremations were carried out in country. One day in the summer of 1968 a Korean woman showed up with her son. The young man had been shot through the elbow in Vietnam severing the ulnar nerve. His fingers looked like a claw, they were not functional. The woman started to scream at me in rapid and accusatory Korean. After the tirade was over I asked a KATUSA who had escorted them to the hospital for a translation. He said the woman was asking me why I didn't go to Vietnam and get shot instead of her son? It was an American war after all. How was he going to do farm work with only one useable hand? I said nothing. What could I say?

One afternoon, about 3:00 P.M., I was getting ready to start my shift. Sgt. Billing came though the barracks door and strode up to me. He looked me directly in the eye and accused me, "You stole a rifle, we have proof."

"What?"

"There is a rifle missing, you were in the arms room the other day and walked off with one."

I said, "What would I do with a rifle?"

He said, "Sell it."

I looked him straight in the eye and said, "You Sorry Lifer. What the hell are you trying to pull?" The remainder of the conversation is lost to time, but I nearly jumped him. I was furious. I walked past him and departed for the hospital. Several days later an SFC approached me and said the rifle had been accounted for. The paper work was found in a cabinet; ordnance had the weapon and was replacing some part. Far from vindication, the sergeants were even more furious than ever. I had insulted one of their own. A lowly Buck Private, yelling at a SFC was unconscionable. It did not occur to these unimaginative men that risking a court-martial and possible dishonorable discharge was not worth the price of an M-14 rifle. The NCO running the arms room could not keep track of his own inventory.

Chapter 5

I was due for an R&R which is given to every G.I. mid-tour. My thoughts turned to a trip to Japan. Kyoto was a national shrine, spared from bombing during WWII on the orders of Henry Stimson, President Roosevelt's Secretary of War, who had visited it as a young man. I packed my AWOL bag. Once I had my orders and took the bus to Kimpo Airport, I began waiting for a flight to Japan. I sat for hours, boredom, no aircraft, no nothing. In the evening of the first day, I departed for ASCOM and I decided to look up Yobo and see if she was up for a little R&R. I explained my idea and she seemed to accept the thought that travel might do us some good. My suggestion was that we go see her parents since she had not seen them for years. The only family she had seen was her sister and brother who resided in Seoul. She took care of the railroad arrangements. While on the platform waiting for the train, a middle age man looked at the gangling American and cute Korean, spat and said something. I asked for a translation, she said, "He say Korean men have no dicks".

The countryside that swept past us was pastoral and flat. Twenty miles outside of Seoul electricity and phone lines disappeared. The homes were mostly thatch roofed and masonry. Wells appeared and the ubiquitous water buffalo worked the rice fields. There were many horse and ox carts visible. I saw a few gasoline powered rice planters and some other modern agriculture implements. Mostly rice farming was labor intensive. Hills and mountains appeared in the distance. We paralleled the coast for many miles. The landscape was broken by inlets of the Yellow sea. The coast appeared to resemble California in the region of Carmel with steep bluffs that dropped off to the sea. Yobo insisted we stop after dark and spend the night in a village "hotel". We slept on straw mats. In the morning the village children met us at the door of the inn. They laughed and pointed at me and made some comments. I asked Yobo what they were saying she giggled and said," They call you giraffe" I guess I was the tallest human being they had ever seen. Some insects had made their home in my scalp overnight but disappeared the next day on board the train. Possibly they did not like the taste of Americans. In the afternoon of the second day, we reached our destination. I knew that in the absence of Yobo my helplessness was complete. I could have been done away with and no one would be the wiser. I completely depended on Yobo for food, shelter and a return ticket to Seoul. The locals could not have been friendlier. The village children turned out whenever I was abroad in the towns. I guess they thought Yobo was my wife. They were always pointing, covering their mouths and laughing. The village elders constantly smiled. They began to appear with cups of wine, and rice cakes. Smiling and bowing. Talk about rolling out the red carpet! I never fully realized how popular Americans were. The forty years of Japanese occupation must have been terrible. I was considered to be an honored guest among them. The Americans had liberated the country in 1945. The older Koreans had not forgotten.

Yobo would get up about 9:00 A.M and insist on washing my feet. What significance this had I did not know. I think it had something to do with rice farming. After a day in the paddy a loyal wife would wash her husband's feet. I was getting the royal treatment. She would disappear about 10:00 or 11:00 A.M. and not return until the late afternoon, I was never invited to the family home and spent most of my time walking around the village. People would smile and nod when they saw me. An American visitor was something unique, possibly I was the first one many of them had ever seen. I felt a little sheepish given that I was traveling with a Korean woman of indeterminate status. When Yobo returned, we would talk about her life as a child. Something interesting emerged. As a young girl she became seriously ill with a very high fever. She was not expected to live but somehow pulled through. Her behavior began to change after recovery. The illness might have been scarlet fever. In her teens she began to have relations with several boys in the village. Sex out of marriage was considered shameful. Her father beat her repeatedly to try to stop the behavior. After taking up with a married man in a neighboring village, her father banished her from home. She journeyed to Seoul and became a prostitute. I think this confession had something to do with her desire to marry and give up the profession. I did not want to marry an Oriental and told her I had hopes to return to the States and finish college.

About the third or fourth day, a local elementary school teacher showed up and asked if I wanted to go hunting with him. I was a little skittish at first wondering if I would be the target, but finally I agreed. He proudly showed me his weapon which was a single shot ancient Iver Johnson 12 gauge shotgun. We trudged up one hill and down another, the terrain was steep and scrub covered. We heard the cackle of pheasants several times, but saw none. He had hand loaded the paper shotgun shells, and used newspaper for wadding. We spent a pleasant day afield and repaired to his home for wine and rice cakes after the safari. The courtesy shown me by this gentleman and his wife is something I remember fondly. As a parting gift Yobo's parents gave me a pair of flannel pajamas. I never met them, but the implication was that I was finally going to make their daughter an honest woman. We boarded the ancient steam powered train and chugged our way back to Seoul. It was a three hundred plus mile journey.

I felt guilty about wasting her time. Cursing my stupidity for getting involved with a whore, I wanted to bow out as quickly as possible. I was still avoiding my fellow GIs and the extra duty roster by sleeping in her hootch. She never asked for money and did her business elsewhere. I was acquainted with others who became involved with the local women. One GI had befriended a tall beautiful prostitute. She was at least five feet ten inches and well proportioned. It turned out that she came from a good family. Her father had gotten into some type of political altercation with officials in the Park regime. He lost his government job and was essentially banned from commerce and industry. The daughter took to the streets to make easy money and aid the family. She spoke passable English and appeared educated. Pregnant by a soldier in our hospital who was in the process of going through all the formidable paper work to effect a marriage. I hope it worked out for them, he seemed to be a good-hearted fellow.

****

By the autumn of 1968 it was becoming evident that the war in Vietnam and the resulting civil unrest were creating real problems for the military. Drug use was on the rise and the draftees were becoming a surly lot, their only interest being returning home in one piece. FTA was making its appearance on barracks walls, doors, and latrines. For a period of time the perpetrators got away with saying it meant fun, travel, and adventure. The real meaning was Fuck the Army. This obviously did not sit well with career NCO's and officers. They began to crack down heavily on these civilian turned soldier miscreants, and put some of the worst offenders in jail. There were more than 200,000 less than honorable discharges given out in the ten year period 1965-1975. Germany was a dangerous place. Those returning from Vietnam or anticipating deployment were virtually powers onto themselves. Senior enlisted men were physically frightened by their subordinates. Sergeants in Germany began to wear side-arms to protect themselves from their own men.
One young specialist that turned up in our barrack said, "I transferred to Korea because I thought it would be safer." 'Fragging' started in Vietnam about this time. The killing of officers and senior enlisted men by short-timers was a consequence of Westmoreland's "We want bodies" strategy. The troops in the field saw the futility of it well before Secretary McNamara did. He quit the Johnson administration when he saw

the hopelessness of the mission. Draftees had no such option.

Some of the NCOs arriving from the States wanted to tighten up the patrols in the DMZ. Due to the large number of line Crossers, ambush patrols were sent out each evening into the DMZ. Eight to twelve men went out with rifles, grenades and M-79 grenade launchers. The ROK army seemed to be engaged in most of the fire fights with the North Koreans, but the 2nd and 7th Infantry Divisions were also on alert The newly arrived SSgt from stateside noticed that the men did not exhibit sufficient neatness and soldierly deportment so he decided to hold A.M. inspections. After being up all night, the troops were unenthusiastic about a full field when they returned from ambush patrols. The EM told the Sergeant that it was SOP to unload weapons in the morning and get to sleep as soon as possible. "Out of the question," stated the SSgt, "we start tomorrow." This went on for a number of days until one specialist stated, "Enough of this Mickey Mouse, we are not going to turn out for any more of your chicken-shit inspections!"

The Sergeant would have none of it. "You do as I say or else!"

The men answered, "Nobody fucks with our sleep! You do this again and we are going to kill you!" Two days later they did just that. The gentleman in question was walking away from a returned patrol and he was shot multiple times in the back with M-14 rifles. He lived for twenty-four hours. Intubated and infused with whole blood, he finally expired. The Sergeant was a real horse.

Malaria was beginning to show up now that the heat of summer was approaching. We were all required to take one quinine derivative pill each morning. Bowls of them were placed in the mess-hall and each of us partook of them. We medics were not supervised during the ingestions. The assumption being that we were more responsible than our infantry brothers. One evening a physician burst through ward C-13 pushing a gurney with a patient in distress. His body temperature was approaching 105

Fahrenheit: a classic case of malaria. The physician was new to the hospital so I did not know him. Apparently the GI in question had just arrived at the E.R. and was diagnosed with malaria. The Doctor said, "Private, get a couple of wash buckets and fill them with ice." We rolled the semi-conscious soldier onto a rubber sheet and I departed the ward. Fortunately, there was an ample supply of cube ice in the freezer and I quickly filled the buckets. Upon returning to the ward, the doctor had already folded up the corners of the of the rubber sheet forming a dam. He said, "Pour ice directly on him, I will hold his shoulders." Dumping both buckets on the kid's chest he levitated. In a scene directly out of "The Exorcist", he went vertical. He broke free of the doctors restraining hands and threw a wild hay maker at me. Luckily, he missed. Two days later he apologized and thanked me for helping him. His recovery was rapid and he was sent back to his unit in less than a week.

Many of the physicians at our hospital were Regular Army. They had received a free medical education with the stipulation that after completion of medical school they would be required to serve five years. I went to central supply one day to get some sheets and pillow cases and a nurse asked me if I would like a cup of coffee. Since it was the end of my shift and late in the evening, I assented. About four surgeons were sitting around shooting the breeze. I remained standing and drank my coffee in silence. The physicians were discussing their residencies and the cases they most remembered. What I heard that evening is burned into my memory. A young Irish surgeon got on the topic of botched abortions. He was a lower middle-class resident of South-Boston and a gifted student. His residency was in a hospital that served the indigent. Early one morning a very attractive nineteen year old girl was wheeled into the OR bleeding profusely from her vagina. She had attempted to terminate her pregnancy with a butcher knife. Despite heroic efforts by the doctors and nurses she succumbed. They all wept. Dr. Dunn then said, "If a pregnant woman does not want to carry a child to term no power on earth will stop her from trying to end it!" This was four years before Roe vs. Wade.

About this time I promised myself that I would try to return to college and complete my degree. These gifted men had inspired me to continue my education. I thought that as a returning veteran, I had a decent shot at getting admitted to a state school. I wrote my mother and asked her to send me an application form for

the University of Illinois. Yobo and I were growing further apart. She still allowed me to sleep in her room, but my visits became more infrequent. It was time to get my act together and try to do something with my life. It was difficult for me to understand how anyone could make the military a career. A rootless nomadic existence who transferred from place to place for at least twenty years. No wonder so many of the senior enlisted men were alcoholics. The loneliness and isolation were palpable. I started to spend more and more time in the library. One of the notable books I remember was the early work of Ernest Hemmingway. He worked for a time on a newspaper and wrote excellent copy. His sparseness as a novelist was probably due to meeting deadlines.

One evening my gaze fell on a recent issue of Army times. Opening the booklet my eyes scanned page after page of field grade officers applying for retirement. The names and ranks were given in the left column and the denials were on the right. I was surprised. Majors and Lieutenant Colonels in shocking numbers were petitioning to leave the Army. In war time, most of the Lieutenants, Captains and Majors were often reserve officers drawn from the ranks of ROTC programs in American colleges and universities. A good percentage of the petitioners for retirement were regular army types. These gentlemen were graduates of West Point. At that moment I realized that the Vietnam War was lost. If career people were throwing in the towel, the die was cast. It is not a good thing for enlisted men to challenge the efficacy of policy. The fact that Lyndon Johnson had in effect resigned months earlier was another harbinger of weakening national resolve. The riots at the Democratic convention in Chicago were not covered in any great detail on Armed forces radio or television. We were all aware of the tumult and rising anti-war feelings of college students. The assassination of Robert Kennedy following so closely on the heels of M.L. King's death had an effect. The country was undergoing a wrenching national debate, and ultimately brought down two Presidents. Looking back on those days my sympathy for Lyndon Johnson is real. As a national leader, he accomplished many notable goals. The Civil Rights legislation, and voting rights laws were long overdue and very courageous. The Vietnam War sullied his reputation. Many years later I learned that after retiring to the LBJ ranch, he returned to his three-pack-a-day smoking. He, in effect, committed slow suicide; the war had destroyed him. I think his proper place in history will one day be realized.

Chapter 6

Central Illinois 1963

After the death of my wounded warrior uncle, Aunt Betty remarried. Her new husband owned a 640 acre farm. I discovered an abandoned quarry on the property and it became my own private swimming hole. It was so isolated that a bathing suit was unnecessary. Skinny dipping was a sensuous feeling. Swimming over the spring fed thermals on a hot day was the closest thing to nirvana a young man could experience. Uncle Lloyd's grandfather had been a union soldier during the Civil War and was shot through the hip at Vicksburg Mississippi. According to my Uncle he never discussed his war experiences with his son or grandson until the very last years of his long life. He had lost so many of his friends the experience was simply blotted out of his memory. As an old man he returned to his youth. I tried to research the record of his regiment but failed. There were many men with the surname Thomas in Illinois, and many regiments in the GAR. The thought of not going into the Army given this family history was simply out of the question. A city boy, such as myself, was amazed at the energy displayed by these old farmers. Up at 5:30, work all day, retire at 9:30, my uncle was indefatigable. My knowledge of farm equipment was very limited, Uncle Lloyd warned me about corn pickers. He said, "These machines harvest corn as well as human limbs. Never get near one when they are in operation!" The combines also needed constant repair. He was always welding a broken turn-buckle or tightening a loose bolt. Uncle Lloyd owned his equipment and would harvest other fields owned by his neighbors. It was a closely knit community. As in most small towns, everyone knew everyone else's business. As an outsider, I found the local ladies were either married or going steady. They would not even talk to you. I was very skittish around women

Anyway: terminally shy. In the autumn, hunting season arrived the first week in November. Pheasants were an Asian import disliked by the farmers. They would eat newly sprouted corn stalks with relish. My uncle gave me permission to shoot both males and females. I never did, but understood his concerns. Corn was money, and the local fauna were cutting into his profits. I admired him for not using inorganic fertilizers. Anhydrous ammonia was just coming into vogue in those days. He claimed with justification that pesticides, herbicides, and fertilizers were ruining the soil. He simply allowed his dairy cattle to relieve themselves in the fields. Natural Fertilizer! The term organic farmer would apply to him. The incidents I describe happened over fifty years ago, but most of his predictions came true. He once said, "The day of the family farm is ending, eventually the banks will own the land." He foresaw agribusiness early on.

****

James M. Gavin commander of the 82nd Airborne Division in WW11 chronicles an incident that occurred at Ft. Benning, Georgia in 1943. Early one morning, Colonel Gavin received a call from the Provost Marshall at the post. A young paratrooper was being held by the MP's for committing a lewd act on the lawn of the court house in neighboring Phenix City, Alabama. Apparently the soldier was vigorously engaged in his work when the young lady's enthusiastic vocalizations caught the attention of the local constabulary. The soldier was arrested and the flower of Southern womanhood released with a stern warning. By the time Gavin reached the Provost Marshal's office, the Post Commander had been alerted and wanted to know what Gavin proposed to do about it. Gavin picked up the phone and told the general, "Considering the fact the young man may be sacrificing his life for his country within the next year, he should be given a medal!" The matter was dropped. One of the reasons General

Terry Allen was relieved from command of the 1st Infantry Division after the Sicilian campaign was his refusal to court martial troops. Generals Patton and Bradley took a dim view of the behavior of his soldiers in Palermo. The wise Chief of Staff General George C. Marshall saved Terry Allen's career. Beloved by his men, General Allen was given a divisional command later in the war.

Bill Mauldin, famous cartoonist of WWII, tells of an incident that happened in Rome after its liberation. Mauldin along with some other soldiers of the 45th Thunderbird division were enjoying some vino at a local café. A young British soldier walked in with full kit complete with a Lee-Enfield rifle. He was clasping the hand of a young Italian woman of about sixteen. He laid down his rifle, pulled down his pants and in the presence of the Americans and British soldiers proceeded to cohabitate with the young lady in the middle of the floor. The patrons were initially astonished, then they broke into applause. Sex was and is as much a part of war as killing. The marital woes of Hollywood stars receive constant scrutiny by the tabloid press. The national pastime may be baseball but the true heart of America is in football. The steroid laced heroes exhibit hyper-masculinity: padded shoulders and tights. Violence: the gladiators are routinely taken off the field in electric carts to be rehabilitated from various injuries. Homo-eroticism: "The tight end is penetrating the end zone!" intones the breathless announcer. This brings us back to Korea.

One night a young GI was having sex with a menstruating prostitute. Somehow he got the bright idea to steal her bloody panties. He returned to the barracks late that night and bided his time until everyone was sleeping. At last the coast was clear, he silently stole over to a sleeping KATUSA and placed the panties delicately over his face. When the Korean awakened the next day he was prepared to kill the practical jokester. I was just coming off the night shift when I beheld the KATUSA storming around the compound carrying an entrenching tool looking for a victim. I had no idea what had transpired, but the look on this young Oriental's face told me to avoid him. How this matter was resolved I do not know. The incident was hushed up, and the offender was never court-martialed.

The court martial that did take place got the offender six months in the 8th Army stockade. Private Doaks felt he was not getting enough time off so he devised an elaborate ruse to defeat the system. He constructed an elaborate dummy to fool the CQ that there was a person sleeping in his bunk. Bed checks as well as drug checks occurred at odd hours to make sure the troops were behaving themselves. Where Pvt. Doaks was storing his dummy remained a mystery. Apparently, he dismantled it in the mornings and secreted it in storage at an unknown location. Unexpectedly, there was a spot drug check in his barracks one night when the inspecting Sergeant nudged the sleeping soldier there was no response. He pulled back the blanket and discovered the pillows and towels that made up the crude dummy. Had it not been for this ruse, Pvt. Doaks would have gotten off with company punishment and a fine. The dummy is what did in the dummy. A summary court-martial was convened and the contrite offender convicted. The company commander had him hauled off in shackles to the stockade. Pvt. Doaks returned to the hospital a week later with a severe eye infection. He had somehow gotten the gonorrheal infection in his eyes. On several occasions he was visible cutting grass, or deepening the compound's ditches. Then one day he simply disappeared. I suppose he was discharged for "conduct unbecoming."

Needless to say, the sexual encounters between the occident and oriental were frequent enough to produce off-spring. These kids were really unfortunate, shunned for their brown hair and blue eyes, their only hope for a decent life was adoption. The Pearl S. Buck foundation did wonderful work in placing these children in adoptive homes. Many found their way to Scandinavia where the Swedes and Norwegians adopted a large number of them. I hope they lived good lives.

Around this time in my service, I awakened one morning

with a swollen face and severe pain in my jaw. For the first and only time in my army career I went on sick call. The ER Doctor was really sharp and sent me directly to the dentist. He inserted a steel probe into my parotid salivary gland and I heard a faint crunch. Apparently a small calculi or stone had formed blocking the gland. My mouth filled with saliva, instant cure. This incident impressed upon me the necessity for higher education. The physicians in our humble hospital knew their craft well.

Later, I was in the PX purchasing some cigarettes and for the first time saw a green beret waiting for the bus to Youngsan. He appeared to be dusty and tanned. Whether he was arriving or departing I never knew. I asked around and found out that there were Special Forces in Korea helping the ROK army hunt down and kill North Korean commandos. They had landed on the east coast and were trying to start a popular uprising against the Park government. The peasants immediately contacted the national police and reported them. All were hunted down and killed. Communism was very unpopular in the south. However, a Green Beret caused an incident that made the German laundryman at ASCOM something of a legend. Rolf Burghoff was a naturalized immigrant who ran the newly installed laundry. He was having a drink at the EM club and a Green Beret Sgt. showed up to tip a few. Burghoff had a limp from some accident earlier in his Army career but was kept on because he was very efficient. The Special Forces man looked at Burghoff and started to mock him. "Hey, look at the gimp, he can't even walk right! Haw Haw. How did you get in the Army, Huh?" At this point Rolf told the "Greenie" to knock it off but he kept it up. "Haw, a Kraut! Get hit in WWII did you?" At this point Rolf invited the loud mouth outside the club to settle matters. The "Greenie" was more than willing to settle the matter outside the club. Apparently his training failed him as Burghoff proceeded to beat hell out of the unfortunate man. Several soldiers stepped in to end the one-sided fight after the defeated "Specialist" failed to get up. I encountered Rolf days later and asked what happened. He stated, "I zlapped the zhit out of the vize mutter fucker." Of such incidents bar room reputations are made. Medals count for something, but bar room reps are everything.

The thefts in the 642 Evac continued, but not all of them were committed by Koreans. Gamma Globulin was an expensive and valued commodity in civilian and military hospitals. Used in immunizations for hepatitis and other diseases it could easily be sold on the black market for good money. It began to disappear along with the frequency of Milk of Magnesia which was also coveted. The difference in price however was significant. An investigation was conducted and a Staff Sergeant who worked in the medical lab was implicated. This gentleman was ultimately court-martialed, reduced in rank, fined and sent north to the DMZ. His career was ruined. The U.S. Army of 1968 was not the Army of 2014. Pay was low and the duty tough. I was not surprised that the Sergeant resorted to theft. He needed the money. I would purchase instant coffee at the PX and sell it to Koreans for a small profit. It was frowned on but everyone did it. By this time my fence climbing escapade was slowly receding from the radar of our enlisted leaders. I was given a new task. Part-time truck driver, but first I had to learn how to drive a truck.

The 642 had an inordinately large motor pool. Upon arrival I asked a mechanic, "Why so many trucks"? He said, "In the event of attack we have orders to load all the hospital equipment and head for Pusan." Apparently the 2nd and 7th infantry divisions were not expected to hold the North Korean juggernaut for more than two days. The Sergeant placed me in the passenger seat and proceeded to instruct me on the gear shift. These were the days prior to the introduction of all automatic transmission vehicles. In WWII, the two and one-half ton truck was a straight-six gasoline engine. The new models were diesel and capable of carrying a much larger payload than their WWII equivalents. Off we went to the training field about five miles away. The training area was at the bottom of an abandoned rock quarry. I took the driver's seat and started the engine. Diesels are far different than gasoline powered vehicles. They must be primed and given some lead time before moving out. The transmissions were fairly easy to manipulate, there were five speeds forward and several in reverse. I pressed the clutch shifted to first and took off. The circumference of the track was about a mile and a quarter.

Round and around we went hour after hour. Whoever designed the course of instruction did not anticipate what real driving entailed. We stopped for a bag lunch around noon. The ROK army also used the course. At about this time a young Korean enlisted man was learning the intricacies of backing up a truck with a water carrier hooked to the rear. The water carrier jack-knifed and slid over the gravel raising a cloud of dust. A senior NCO wrenched open the door of the vehicle and yanked the poor enlisted man out. He exploded in a rage of Korean expletives and started kicking the poor man very hard. By this time the scene was attracting attention, screaming in pain the poor private began crying and pleading for mercy. Finally the beating stopped and the Sergeant walked away muttering to himself about the miserable "Pabos" he had to work with. This was an object lesson in the "discipline" meted out to under-performing enlisted men in the ROK army. Non-commissioned officers had tremendous power over their subordinates. Such actions would not be tolerated in the U.S. Army.

After this episode I decided driving around in circles was beginning to get boring so I decided to take a trip. There was a gravel path to a lower level of the quarry that was unused. I decided to test my prowess in down shifting by leaving the track and going to the lower level. I had negotiated about half the distance to the bottom of the quarry when "boom!" I blew a tire. An NCO from our own company ran over and proceeded to berate my family lineage for daring to deviate from the curriculum. I had difficulty suppressing a laugh. The tire should not have gone flat as I was not stressing it excessively. At any rate I wound up having to change it which was not easy. Especially, the jacking-up part. The powers that be thought this was sufficient punishment and I was not charged for the damage. Needless to say, I did not get my driver's license.

I was still working the night shift which was fine with me. I wanted to terminate the relationship with Yobo and this provided the perfect excuse. We drifted apart. One night in early September the O.D. ran into the ward about 1:30 A.M. and said I was needed in the O.R. I said, "Nurse Pace and I are the only ones covering two wards with about forty patients, she cannot work here alone." "This is an order private, Get Moving!" I entered the O.R. and beheld a surgeon laboring over the open abdomen of a gunshot soldier. There had been another shooting in the DMZ. Besides the anesthesiologist and the Doctor, no surgical nurses or medics were in evidence.

"Where is everyone?" I asked.

The physician replied "Put on some surgical gloves and give me a hand." It turned out that a North Korean soldier had cranked off a round in the dark and the unlucky G.I. received the lucky shot in the abdomen. A rifle shot in the stomach can be lethal. This bullet had been fired at considerable distance because there was no exit wound. The Doctor was stitching up numerous holes in the pinkish small intestine, and asked me to help look for more perforations. I was very reluctant to even approach the wounded man. I had not scrubbed or put on a sterile surgical gown. Carefully donning latex gloves, I timidly grasped the small intestine and moved it slightly to search for more damage. Some of the contents of the gut had leaked out into the abdominal cavity and the doctor instructed me to pour in some saline solution so the food could be suctioned out. I discovered the bullet resting on a fold of the intestine. It had the characteristic shape of a high velocity AK round. I removed it with the aid of a mosquito hemostat and placed it in a small jar. It was, now, evidence in an unprovoked attack on U.S. troops in the DMZ. By this time additional back up arrived and I was able to go back to my assigned ward. It remains a mystery to me why I was called in the first place. The absence of a surgical nurse or operating room tech remained a puzzle. The young man survived, and there was no post- op infection.

Recreation or physical training was lacking overseas. Other than the boudoir athletics practiced by the enlisted men and officers, we were not "combat ready". Higher powers decided that our gin-soaked, debauched bodies needed a little toning. The regimen began with daily calisthenics followed by a morning run. This went on for several weeks until the testing day arrived. We were given the same physical fitness test as administered in basic training. It took two attempts but I finally passed. My weight had increased by twenty pounds since basic training. The hospital menu was not great but I could always take food off the trays of the patients too sick to eat. The poor infantry types were stuck with cold C-rations. We resumed our lives of indolence pending the possibility of yet another round of physical training.

****

July 1970

I was leisurely driving down the street one afternoon nearing my home when a car whizzed by and cut me off. I was doing the limit and this individual seemed oblivious to the fact he was speeding toward a red light. I tapped my horn and the driver stuck his hand out of the window and flipped me the bird. To add insult to injury, he reached the stop light and purposely braked too quickly. Apparently he was trying to get me to hit him. Big mistake! I jumped out of my Volkswagen ran up to his car wrenched open the door and grabbed him by his collar. I threw him against the side of the car and began slapping him hard. There were two other young men in his auto but they made no attempt to help him. I remember distinctly my vision had turned pink. I guess I continued to slap him and slam him against the side of the car for a while. By this time the light had changed to green but I was oblivious. A truck driver pulled up and started to yell at me, "You had better stop, fella, you are getting into a lot of trouble!" This brought me back to reality. I ran back to my car jumped in and took off.

The extent of my trouble became apparent the next day. The Hickory Park Police Chief called my home and wanted to "Speak to me about the incident." I knew if I showed up at the station I would be arrested for battery. Legal advice was sought. I phoned an attorney who was related to a friend of mine from high school and he said he would make inquiries. He stated, "Under no circumstances should you go to the police station, they will most certainly detain you." A day later Attorney Goss phoned me and stated, "You really got yourself into trouble, the fellow you assaulted was the nephew of the Chief of Police. Under no circumstances should you drive through Hickory Park. They have your license number. If you stay out of the community, they will have to issue a warrant for your arrest through the Cook County State's Attorney. Did you hurt the young man badly?"

Reluctantly, I answered, "I doubt it, I just slapped him around." Thank God for the legal profession. I stayed out of Hickory Park for the next three years. I was never served with a warrant.

It was obvious to me I had some anger management problems. I was now finishing my junior year at the University of Illinois. I had to maintain a "B" average or I would lose probation and be expelled. I really hit the books, dropping out for a second time would have been too bitter to contemplate. I graduated one year later and began my teaching career; it lasted thirty-three years. I met my wife at the University which worked out well, forty-three years and counting. Deciding after careful evaluation of my behavior, yours truly became a law-abiding citizen and never experienced further problems with the law. I have struggled with nightmares for years and have great difficulty finding and holding friends.

****

In the early autumn, we went on periodic alerts. The rumored release of the Pueblo was making the rounds and we had to prepare for the arrival of eighty-three men. There was no information on the condition of the sailors, but it can be surmised that the Geneva Convention was not being observed. It was very difficult to negotiate with the North Koreans. They demanded apologies from the U.S. government as well as the Captain of the ship. One must remember, no formal treaty was ever signed with the Northerners; there was a cease fire in 1953 but nothing more. America was considered to be the "capitalist aggressor responsible for the death of Robert Kennedy who wanted to make peace" and the South Koreans were "the running dogs of the imperialist Americans". What really destroyed the negotiations was the appearance in Time magazine of East German photos showing the captive Americans with their index fingers raised. The sailors told the Koreans that this was the Hawaiian good luck sign. The editors of Time knew better and labeled the raised fingers an "obscene gesture". When this information reached the DPRK there was hell to pay, but more about that later.

More soldiers were arriving from Vietnam on a monthly basis. Many were under the impression that once they arrived in Korea they could relax and let their hair down. Alcohol and Bupyong did not mix. One evening, when I was again on the extra duty roster, a call came in to the emergency room. There was an unconscious GI in a ditch just outside the compound. I walked down the hill from the helipad and passed the M.P at the gate. There were a group of Korean civilians staring down into a gully apparently unwilling to get involved. We walked over to the small crowd and peered down into the depression. There was a middle-age sergeant unconscious staring with unseeing eyes into the gathering evening gloom. His pockets had been pulled out and he bore the appearances of someone who had put up a brief but gallant fight. Fortunately, I had an emergency bag with ampoules of ammonia. With some difficulty we managed to bring him around, but he had obviously suffered a concussion. His speech was slurred and he seemed to be unsure of exactly where he was. I decided it might be a good idea to call for a stretcher as I was unsure whether he could make it back to the hospital under his own power. Luckily, my decision was sound, the neuro-surgeon, Dr. Levine, determined SFC Odom had suffered a concussion as well as a cerebral hematoma with some bleeding. It took him a week to recover.

This incident was a stern warning to the troops that the 'friendlies' could turn mercenary when they smelled money and drink. The condition of many of the NCOs that I saw in the Army led me to a life of sobriety. I only, occasionally, drink wine and seldom drink beer as a consequence. Another example of the effects of "Demon Rum" was SSgt Tourre. The sergeant had returned from Vietnam and chose to come to Korea. He had a girlfriend and there was really no reason to return to America. One day, he complained of feeling light-headed and ill. Some routine tests were performed and it was found Tourre had elevated white blood cell levels indicating leukemia. Further tests were administered and the diagnosis was changed: Acute alcohol toxicity. The poor man was so unnerved by his experiences in Vietnam, his intake of alcohol became excessive even by Army standards. No ticket home for Sgt Tourre. He had to dry out overseas.

A combat engineer came in one day with severe diabetes aggravated by alcoholism. The senior NCO was a proud WWII veteran and a talker. His proudest achievement in WWII was his work with mines and booby-traps. He was involved in the liberation of Naples and Rome. The Germans always left their departing calling-cards in the form of the afore mentioned devices. Sgt. Davis had to deal with an especially devilish invention called a "butter-fly" bomb. These explosives were dropped from aircraft and were armed by spinning vanes on each side which deployed after the small cylindrical bomblets burst from their casing. This, in effect, was the first use of a so-called "cluster bomb" They were extremely sensitive and if picked up would immediately explode.

Initially they were detonated by rifle fire from about seventy-five yards. This was not a practical solution in an urban environment. People could be killed by ricochets. Sandbags were placed around them, and a small charge was tossed in to detonate them. This proved too time-consuming. Sgt. Davis came up with the perfect solution: fill a dump truck with sand, upend the load directly over the bomb-lets and they immediately blew up. It was fast, effective and a non-time consuming solution to the problem. The sergeant got a medal for his idea which was not an insignificant contribution to the war effort. He told me other stories but this is the one that remains clear in my memory.

Alas, not all my patients were as pleasant to deal with as Sgt. Davis. I had to work in the isolation unit from time to time. One had to mask, gown and glove and enter the ward with cloth shoe covers. Osteo tuberculosis is virtually unknown in industrialized countries, but this, however, is not the case in third world nations. I have always been a supporter of the World Health Organization. This is one program that The United Nations administers well. Former President Carter's heroic efforts to eliminate the Guinea Worm in Africa is another example. The exact reason this Korean man was admitted into an Army hospital escapes me. He must have had political connections. Whatever the reason, I had to care for him. Moving him for any reason, use of the bedpan, eating, or placing him in a wheel chair was agony. His screams were terrible. The poor man had no chance of surviving but his last months were a miasma of pain and suffering.

Worse still was gas-gangrene. Fortunately, I only had to deal with this condition once. Government employees were often admitted into the hospital due to a lack of better facilities elsewhere. The gentleman that I dealt with had advanced diabetes and peripheral artery disease. This translates into a lack of circulation in the extremities. His toes were literally rotting; why the amputation was not done immediately mystified me. Suffice to say, dressing his feet was another assignment given to yours truly. The nurses wanted no part of this task and neither did I. The odor arising from his feet made me nauseous. I could only imagine the hell of trench warfare in WWI without antibiotics.

I have spoken of the respect I had for the majority of physicians and nurses, unfortunately there were others. Major Fred Reserve was another draftee Physician. When he received his "Greetings" message from General Hershey he made it clear that a Captaincy in the Army Medical Corps was not good enough. He wanted the golden leaves of a Major! Incredibly he got his wish. But was Major Reserve satisfied with his instant promotion? No way. He constantly bitched and moaned about all the money he was losing while working for Uncle Sam. He routinely was seen walking the halls of the 642 pissing and moaning about the $100,000 per year he was losing when he left his lucrative civilian practice in Kansas. Remember folks, these were 1968 dollars! Fortunately, this gentleman was the exception to the rule. I am not so sure the present group of healthcare professionals are as altruistic as their elders were. Excluding the financial factor, there was a good deal of rivalry among the physicians regarding their proficiency as surgeons. An unofficial pecking order existed among them. The regular Army LTC that ran the hospital was scoffed at by his much younger peers. Completing a surgical procedure in as little time as possible is still the mark of a good surgeon. The longer a wound is open, the greater the chance of post-operative infection. The 642 had an excellent record because less than 4% of the patients suffered post-op problems. LTC Time-Warp never kept his eye on the clock. In fact, he was noted for his meticulous and time-consuming suturing. One of the few times he performed a procedure, a not too simple appendectomy, the big hand of the O.R. clock was well past one hour and he was still going strong. The nurses and medics just shook their heads. But who among them was going to offer any suggestions to a Lt. Colonel?

One day, I was just coming on duty for the routine night-shift when I spotted a Master Sergeant sitting at the admissions desk. Every SFC I knew lusted after that third rocker. It was a big jump from Sergeant First Class to Master Sergeant and many of the enlisted men would have tied their grandmothers to railroad tracks in order to gain the elusive third rocker. I thought it unusual that a senior E.M. would be doing the work of a Buck Sergeant or a Spec/4 for that matter. I shrugged it off and reported for duty. Several days later I came on duty and again saw him at the desk with his head lowered in deep thought. By this time I was curious and made some polite inquiries. It turned out the gentleman was having serious psychological problems. He was removed from Vietnam due to severe migraines and the inability to sleep. He requested to be sent to Korea to complete his twelve month tour overseas. Apparently, the methods being employed to subdue the Vietcong were alien to his rural Southern Baptist upbringing. Recon by fire is what ultimately caused his

mental breakdown. The Master Sergeant was a senior enlisted medic in a Cavalry Unit. In those days the armored forces in Vietnam routinely rode around the countryside in M-113 armored personnel carriers. It was common to stop well out-side of a village and fire the .50 caliber machine gun over the roofs of the hootches. If fire was returned, even one round directed at the Americans, the village was considered hostile and was leveled. The afore-mentioned Sergeant could not deal with this tactic. It was an assault on their livelihoods and innocents were routinely killed. He served in the rear for a period of time in Vietnam, but his memories of the carnage happening all around made him a liability. He kept his rank and was quietly spirited out of the country.

As mentioned earlier the 8th Army Stockade routinely supplied work parties to keep the compound neat and clean. Many of these men had their hands shackled and used brooms, shovels, and paint brushes to tidy up. The MP companies were not noted for harboring any Mother Theresas and they often treated their prisoner charges with contempt and cruelty. It is never wise to insult a prisoner who is holding a shovel. I did not see the incident, nor did I see the MP when he was admitted to the hospital, but I saw a black and white photo taken when he was carried in. The prisoner cracked and threw a wild swing at the MP with his shovel, it caught the unfortunate full in the face. His nose was completely flattened, both orbits of his eyes were broken, all of his front teeth were knocked out, and his skull was fractured. The amazing thing was he was still alive. He was stabilized and shipped directly to Japan. I doubt that the medical facility at Camp Zama could have helped him much more than the Mayo Clinic.

Chapter 7

February 2003

"The principal would like to see you after school Mr. Sirkin," said the student office aide. In my thirty odd years of teaching, I had never received a verbal message from the front office. Normally evaluations were set up well in advance and delivered in letter form. Immaculate Miracle High School was located in Irving, Illinois about thirty-five miles from Chicago. I still had two more classes before the day ended, and had two hours to contemplate the request. I sat in the outer office for about twenty minutes waiting to be summoned by the principal. Finally I was ushered in and offered a chair. The principal asked, "Would you like a cup of coffee, Mr.Sirkin?" I said, "Yes." She contemplated me for a moment and began, "You have a very good reputation at the school, the students always ask the guidance counselor to be placed in your Biology or Chemistry classes. I have never faulted your judgment or professionalism until recently. Why are you politicizing your students?" I was a bit taken aback by this statement but inquired as to how she came to this conclusion. "You have made some derogatory statements about the President and Vice President."

I answered, "Yes, I have"

"Why?" she said.

"Because I think the President and Vice President are working very hard to convince the American people that the Iraq War is necessary."

The Principal stared at me for a moment and said, "A parent phoned me and was quite upset, she said that you mentioned that we were only interested in oil."

"That is correct." I said.

"Mr.Sirkin, I am placing you on probation. Any further comments on this subject and you will be terminated, is that clear?"

"Yes Ma'am." I said. (So much for free speech.)

Socrates or Aristotle once said, "A mind is not a vessel to be filled, rather a fire to be lit." Needless to say, my army career did not turn me into a conservative. I was always lighting fires of one sort or another. The teaching career generally does not draw risk-takers. Most of them did very well in school. They were officers in the student council, pom-pom girls, Future Homemakers of America and so on. In other words, rocking the boat was unthinkable. They were pulling the oars or rather guiding the tiller. I had the ability to tell a story and make my students laugh. It is much easier to teach by using humor rather than earnestness. One memorable student-teacher open house remains clear. A parent came to me with a unique story. The father was a graduate chemist who had gone on to law school. He was a patent attorney and could not understand why his daughter hated her middle school science teachers. When she began as a freshman biology student with me, the father reported, she never stopped talking about my class. It was her favorite. He thanked me profusely for this turn-around. The young lady ultimately graduated Phi Beta Kappa from The University of Chicago. In my last ten years of active teaching, I have appeared in "Who's Who of American Teachers" four times. Did this performance garner any respect from my colleagues? It actually worked against me. How can this former college drop-out be so popular? Ultimately my students began quoting me in other classes. But Mr. Sirkin said thus and so you must be incorrect. The woman who taught advanced biology and picked up one beginning class in biology was only too aware of my popularity. Every bit of graffiti on the desks, every over-filled pencil sharpener reservoir, was attributed to me.

One year we were dissecting sharks, the specimens were several years old, and the odor was unbearable. Since it was late spring, I decided to go outside the school and use the aluminum stadium bleachers as surfaces upon which to place the dissecting trays. The students were squeamish about the dissection in the first place, but this, coupled with the horrific odor, was too much for some. I excused a number of the kids from the work since I did not wish to make them physically ill. My colleague would have none of it. She insisted I return to the classroom and do the work "where it was supposed to be done!" I politely told her to mind her own business. Not satisfied, she took the matter to the principal. When I explained the situation to the administrator and I allowed her to examine one of the odoriferous sharks she agreed with my decision. Mrs. Rote was not a fan of mine, but this situation just added to her hatred of me. I think the basis of her discomfort stemmed from the fact I was from a working class background. Her husband was a successful lawyer and a prominent force in the community. I decided to keep quiet and bore my discomfort in private. The real reason, I later learned, was that the students wanted me to take over the advanced biology classes. I was "funny" while Mrs. Rote was most definitely not.

Even though I spent half of my career as a public school teacher, and half at parochial schools, by the latter half of the nineties testing was beginning to be the be all and end all of education. SAT scores flat lined in the mid 80's and rather than accept the fact that students were getting neither, smarter nor dumber and that flat scores should be expected, they changed the test. Onward the sine curve had to go up and up. This softened the hearts of the genius politicians who guide our collective destinies. In the inner cities, where scores had been lagging or dropping over the years, a reason had to be found for failure. The children can't be blamed, or the poverty, or the broken homes, or the street crime. Where are the villains? Answer: Why they are in our midst. It's the incompetent and lazy teachers with their three month vacations and overly generous pensions who are responsible. Enter the education experts from stage right. Bill Bennett was the man of the hour. This "Patrician" could solve any problem. Drugs? Education? He's your man. The tweedy types from Yale and Harvard declared in unison, "Money doesn't matter in public education" This from elites who never set foot in a public school. Choate and Phillips Exeter Academy do not come cheap. From a political party that wants to get rid of the Department of Education and the Environmental Protection Agency, all this makes good sense. Public Education is a menace and Teacher's Unions are the enemy. Public schools and land grant universities built the United States of America. Now we have to replace it with something better. The something better is charter schools and for profit education.

Since money means nothing in education, it makes sense that the Superintendents of these entities vote themselves huge salaries. One Charter School Chief is currently earning a whopping salary of $528,280 per annum. While the average public school teacher makes about $64,000 annually at the top of the pay scale after twenty years on the job. Collectively, about $500 billion in tax dollars is pumped into Public Education each year. It is no accident that the Wall Street hustlers want to get their greedy fingers into all this cash. Look no further than the Bush family. One Of H.W. Bush's children is heavily involved in the charter school industry. Make no mistake, there is money in "them thar" books and educational materials. George W. Bush famously said, "The question is: Is our children learning?" This hustler did more to undermine Public Education in America than any Teacher. No Child Left Behind is quietly being abandoned by most states.

Is the current occupant of the White House any more enlightened? I doubt it. His current Education Czar is not asking any hard questions. Where is the empirical proof? Mark Twain once gave a classic rejoinder to the idea of a gold mine. He said, "A gold mine is a hole in the ground with a liar at the bottom." The reformers of education in this country might well look into the money trail and the number of charter school students who are dumped back into public education if they are trouble makers or low achievers. The snake oil salesmen of the 19th century could learn a thing or two from the current crop of education reformers.

****

Verdun France 1999

One does not need to go to Africa to witness Conrad's The Heart of Darkness. It is on permanent display in France. Civil War battlefields in America are rather unimposing relics of a bygone era. There are no craters from bombs or artillery, rather one is greeted by imposing granite monuments to regiments or companies. Heroic statues of infantrymen using their rifles as clubs to slay the Yankees or Rebels are visible but little else. Verdun lacks such heroic bronzes. The horror is visible in the earth. It is still dangerous to walk the killing fields. The pock-marked soil is green and over-grown, but the specter of death lingers. I thought my experiences in the Army had hardened me but the massive ossuary where the bones of 100,000 unidentified gallant Frenchmen are interred still shocks. World War II is now referred to as the Holocaust. But it should be referred to as Holocaust II. Poison gas, millions of rounds of explosives hurled at the opposing enemy and a landscape torn and rendered virtually uninhabitable greet every visitor. Anyone who doubts the gallantry of the French Army need only witness Verdun. I had decided to journey to the Argonne forest to visit the approximate location of the 33rd Illinois infantry division of which my Uncle was a member. Stopping in Verdun almost concluded my tour.

Eric Maria Remarque understood there was a generation of men who physically survived WWI but were destroyed by it. Hemmingway wrote of it: "The Lost Generation". My own terrible temper and inability to relate to other adults might have been my helper in teaching children. They thought I was funny but the humor I displayed masked a darker side. My family saw it, my students didn't. War exposes the Janus of our souls: Nobility and

Baseness, Heroism and Cowardice, Love and Hate. In the forty-five years that have elapsed since my separation from the Army I never met a group of men I liked more.

By 1917, the French Army had reached its nadir. Static warfare had drained any "elan" that remained among the troops. "Allez Le Enfants Pour France" was long gone. The soldiers began to mutiny.

The Generals: American, British and German, feared a return to static warfare. It almost happened in Normandy in June and July of 1944. The break-out prevented this situation. Unfortunately for the soldiers in WWI, there was no Air Force to open a corridor. The French were willing to lose men defending a position but refused to attack. This was beginning to happen in Vietnam. Soldiers on patrol would move out at night and phone in phony coordinates to indicate they were following a patrol sector. It is a terrible feeling to fight over the same ground repeatedly never really holding anything. The enemy ruled the night and the initiative was always with them. We were losing. Years later it was determined that something on the order of 80% of fire fights in Vietnam were initiated by the other side. We were fighting a defensive shadow war with the North Koreans, the difference? Their southern cousins wanted no part of Communism.

What amazed and astounded me in the run up to the 2003 war with Iraq was the almost giddy response of the press corps. It was the first battle of 1861 all over again, Bull Run with tanks and jet fighters. A local reporter from Chicago was with the first troops crossing the border from Kuwait to Iraq. It was like the Super Bowl. All that was missing were pompon girls and a picnic lunch. Had we so quickly forgotten what war was really like? After living with me for over twenty-five years my son joined me in an anti-war parade in Chicago. It was in early March 2003 in below zero temperatures. Thousands of people marched down State Street protesting the rush to invade. The media barely reported the demonstrations. It was a long drive to Chicago and back home but I had to do it. The arms inspections had resumed and it seemed to me that the situation could be defused through negotiations.

When Bush appeared on the aircraft carrier in the famous "flight suit sequence", I knew he was a total fraud. Can you imagine Woodrow Wilson or FDR participating in such an obscene stunt? If Generalissimo Bush was trying to pass himself off as a combat vet, the image of the victorious pilot came back to haunt him. But reflection or guilt was not a part of the George W. Bush persona. The man was completely amoral. An empty suit! During the re-election campaign of 2004 he besmirched the reputation of a real combat veteran. John Kerry was held up as a fraud to the American people. They pilloried the wrong man.

Speaking of politics, the 1968 Presidential Campaign was in full swing. As stated before, the military is predominately conservative, rural and southern. The common refrain around the hospital was "Dump the Hump". Hubert Humphrey, the erstwhile presidential candidate of 1960, was at it again. This time he bore the onus of Vietnam, as vice-president under Lyndon Johnson. Sgt. Helborn was most firm in his opinion, "Ain't but one man runnin' for President, George Corley Wallace!" What else would you expect from an Alabamian? We had a number of college grads in the unit, and they were reading Norman Mailer's The Armies of The Night. There were several of these books circulating among the enlisted men. No one complained because most of the professional military enlisted people did not know who Norman Mailer was and would have guessed he was a postal worker. The hospital library had one copy of the Human Sexual Response by Masters and Johnson. It was kept in a locked glass cabinet. The kicker was only officers could check it out! The army could not deal with the idea of single men having sex. Reading about it might arouse them.

SSgt Harry Overstreet was a new arrival in the 642 Hospital. He had spent a year in Vietnam. Drafted in 1952 and seeing active duty as an infantryman in Korea, he had an ugly scar visible on his right arm. He had been shot during a Chinese attack near Uijeonbu. Harry was quite a character; he made it quite clear that he was getting out of the Army in 1972. Twenty years in service and a pension. He did not like the 642 and repeatedly referred to the Hospital as, "This chicken fuckin' outfit." I asked him why, if he disliked the army so much, he remained in service? His answer remains vivid in my memory. "Who would hire a black man in Tennessee with a right arm that has no strength in it?" This is why the army kept him on as a medic. Harry had completed his tour in Vietnam and was at Ton San Nuet Airport, waiting for a flight out of the Nam in February 1968. The airfield was being rocketed and mortared. Planes were unable to take off and land. A Vietnamese soldier guarding the field lost it and turned his Thomson Sub-machine gun on the waiting Americans. Three were killed and a number wounded. You will not see this bit of history in any book on the Vietnam War. Harry was understandably disgusted by his experiences.

The Forth Estate was considerably more credible during the Vietnam War. Superb journalists like David Halberstam and Neil Sheehan laid bare the contradictions and lies perpetrated by the military in the early sixties. The journalists of the day coined the term "credibility gap" in reference to President Johnson's statements regarding progress in the conflict. Few offered up any criticism in the run up to the second Iraq war. Some brave souls did, but their comments were discredited or ignored. After 9/11 the American people wanted blood, they got it. There are no Walter Cronkites today.

****

University of Chicago 1989:

I was a participant in a fellowship program for teachers of Chemistry at the University the summer of Tiananmen Square. The response of the students was heartening. I had not seen such concern and outrage since the Sixties. The students and faculty were so intelligent and involved with our progress we all worked very hard. The classes consisted of duplications of some of the great experiments of bygone days as well as synthesis of newly discovered compounds. Luciferin was the compound that caused fireflies to glow. The ubiquitous "light sticks" seen at Fourth of July fireworks shows was, at that time, the latest rage. We had to synthesize the compound in class. Not an easy task. I spent the better part of a day working on the molecule. Upon completion of the synthesis, I entered the dark room, nothing, no glow was visible. I dejectedly entered the lab crestfallen at my failure. "What's wrong?" inquired the grad assistant.

"I must have made a mistake somewhere in the protocol, it doesn't glow."

"Shake up the flask," she said. I did, it worked. "Success snatched from the jaws of failure." It was no accident that the U of C was chosen as the site for the first sustained fission reaction. The scientists at the school were first rate, I am still humbled today by the experience.

****

The reasonable man attempts to adapt himself to society as he finds it. The unreasonable man attempts to adapt society to his own lights. Therefore all human progress depends on unreasonable men. Jesus, Gandhi, Galileo, M.L. King, Rachel Carson, Linus Pauling were all unreasonable. Rachel Carson was one of my early heroes. Her seminal work <u>The Silent Spring</u> was published the year of my graduation from high school, 1962. The vilification she endured at the time was disgusting. She was accused of being a Communist, a lesbian, an unqualified "bird watcher", you name it. She was ultimately vindicated. DDT was banned, but what happened after her death in 1964? Back to business as usual, the use of potent herbicides in Vietnam and Korea led to a host of cancers and birth defects in the children of veterans. The new elephant in the room is depleted uranium munitions. Uranium is heavier than lead and was used in Iraq to penetrate the cement walls of homes in Ramadi. Birth defects and cancers are beginning to show up there. The South Korean government is now suing the United States for damages resulting from the use of Agent Orange in the DMZ during the 1960's. The empty drums were buried without notifying the local authorities. The use of Agent Orange was a closely kept secret until 1994. Many have been carelessly exposed to that toxin.

I have dwelt a good deal on the more lurid aspects of Army life. There were upsides. One of the ward masters I came to know, was a genuine hero. He sported a purple heart with oak leaf cluster on his class "A" uniform: two combat wounds! What I did not know was one was received in the Second World War, and the other in Korea. SFC Owens had enlisted in the Army in 1944 at the ripe age of sixteen. As he put it to me, "My brothers were all in the service, I felt lonely." He got to Europe in Late October 1944. I asked him how he managed to avoid discovery as a teenager. He said the manpower shortage late in the war was so severe no one asked any questions. Owens was a large heavy set man and it was easy to imagine him passing for a nineteen year old. He handled a Browning Automatic Rifle or BAR in the military and was assigned to the 4th Infantry Division. Just a few days into the Bulge he was wounded by mortar fire in Belgium. He said smiling, "I could not have found Belgium on a map in those days." After a week and a half in hospital he was sent back into the lines still wearing bandages. After the war he re-enlisted and spent the next several years in the Army of occupation in Germany. When the Korean War started he was immediately sent to Japan and then helped defend the Pusan perimeter in 1950. After the Inchon Landings, the North Koreans retreated north to the Yalu River. The 8th Army was in hot pursuit. In October 1950, Chinese volunteers entered the conflict. The Army was sent reeling to the South in a pell-mell retreat. By now Owens was assigned to a cavalry unit. In the headlong retreat south he was fortunate to be a passenger in a deuce and one-half truck. It mounted a .50 caliber machine gun. The driver yelled at the passengers to lie down in the bed of the truck as they had to run a gauntlet of intense small arms fire in order to make good their escape. They obeyed. Somehow a live grenade was tossed into the back of the truck. It exploded near the soldier next to him who absorbed the full blast, The concussion was so severe both of Owen's ear drums were shattered. He was placed on limited duty for the remainder of the war and ultimately became a medic. I asked him how he could endure yet another war, his third. He never answered.

Another combat vet who was assigned to our hospital was an African American named Wright. SSgt Wright was another infantryman turned medic. I asked him what his most memorable experience was from the Korean War. He said, "I had short legs and could not run fast enough." I asked him what had happened. "We were in the process of being overrun by a Chinese company, our orders were to hold but it was impossible. I had my M-1 but was a little late in retreating. By this time, the Chinks was behind us. My bayonet was fixed and I started to run. Almost immediately I collided with a Chinese soldier carrying a burp gun. I bayoneted him in the chest and tried to pull my rifle out but couldn't so I just dropped it and ran."

"How did you manage to make it?" I asked.

"I don't know, they might have slowed down to kill some of our wounded."

One morning I was just getting off duty and was passing the O.R. when a medic emerged in scrubs and handed me a large white plastic bag he said, "Run this up to pathology will you?" I nodded and he handed the bag to me. It was quite heavy. I started up the hill toward the helipad and the medical records/pathology hut. I stopped and took out a cigarette from my breast pocket and lit it. I decided to open the bag and see what was inside. There were two amputated legs. What I noticed was they were different, one was very hairy, the other wasn't. Two different men! I wondered if they had stumbled into one of our own minefields, or one planted by the North Koreans. I dropped off the bag with the NCOIC and went back to my barracks to get some sleep.

Yobo and I had pretty much gone our separate ways and I had no desire to strike up a new relationship. I went to see her one day and we repaired to a local restaurant to get something to eat. She mentioned her parents had sent her a letter thanking me for the trip south. They had not seen her in years. I believe Yobo was about thirty years old at the time, I was twenty-four. I kissed her and said see you later. We parted. My thoughts were turning toward my career possibilities. Somehow I had to get a degree. Being an enlisted man in the Army had taught me an important life lesson. Without a credential you were doomed to a life of thankless toil. One of my off-duty nights was interrupted by screaming and yelling from a neighboring barrack. I knew it could not be the Hillbilly going crazy again. His quarters were much further away. Someone else had gone bonkers. I had no desire to go out and take a look. The next day the news was all over the compound. An enlisted man had received two letters several days apart. The first was a "Dear John letter". Mrs. Swivel loved her darling husband dearly but it was time to move on so she would not be waiting for him to return. Sp/4 Swivel had received a second letter from his cousin saying that his dear wife was screwing his best friend, a civilian. This was too much to bear. He wound up being restrained by two stretchers: one underneath, one on top, secured by canvas straps. A human sandwich! He continued to scream all the way to the psych ward.

Speaking of the psych ward, the day nurse had taken up with an enlisted man. In the Army, officers having carnal knowledge of each other was common so long it was a heterosexual relationship. But an officer and a lowly enlisted man was heinous! They were both very nice kids and fancied themselves as potential flower children back in the U.S. The female officer was told in no uncertain terms to desist in their trysts. They both pledged to end the relationship, but cleverly changed the venue. They made arrangements with a local madam to use unoccupied rooms in the ville' to continue the affair. Everyone was happy. They eventually got married. I hoped they lived happily ever after.

Not all female officers pledged their troth to only one man. Lt. Vonetta Climax liked to play the field. She was also noted for her proclivity to demand sex in different positions. Many different positions! Lt. Climax would not have attracted much attention walking down the street in hometown U.S.A. She was plain in looks and wide in girth but made up for it in many intriguing ways. I believe she could have added several chapters to the Kama Sutra. Still waters, as they say, run deep. Her paramour was a dark Columbian immigrant who liked to talk. Did he like to talk! He would regale the troops with stories of his experiences with Lt. Climax. Apparently they had it off in the broom closet one night. He timed it, three minutes. Another young nurse, Lt. Inchoate Orifice was also fond of enlisted men. Her claim to fame was a powerful vagina that could clamp down on the male organ and virtually stop intercourse in its tracks. Her musculature was a subject of awe and mystery. How did she do it? Exercise? Concentration? Communion with God? No one had a valid theory.

One night all the female hospital staff descended on the showboat lounge en masse. The bar girls were not happy, non-professionals were not welcome. Especially American girls who were massive compared to their Korean opposite numbers. They were subject to elbows in the rib cage. Spike heels on their feet, dirty looks, and even head butts. After an hour or so they beat a retreat never to return. Whether any of the escapades of these women ever reached the ears of the hospital commander, I do not know. Suffice to say, if they could hear what was being said about them their ears would have turned red.

Vietnam did not directly affect us other than the lack of manpower and equipment. There were rumblings that major changes were in the wind. William Childs Westmoreland, the commanding General in RVN, was a bit of an enigma. Beetle browed with a jutting chin and immemorial gaze, the West Point graduate was a non-descript artillery officer in WWII. His aide-de-camp was Otto Kerner who went on to become Governor of Illinois. At the conclusion of the War in Europe, Westy realized he was going nowhere fast. He switched branches, Airborne all the way. His career took off. It is often said all armies fight the last war all over again. The Maginot line in eastern France is a monument to that precept. The French believed that a second war with Germany would follow the trajectory of WWI. The Germans in 1940 had different ideas. Westmoreland fought the Vietnam War much as he had lived WWII: 'hammer and anvil' tactics to squeeze the enemy into a kill zone, and massive use of artillery and tactical air power. You do not win hearts and minds by destroying the livelihoods of the people you have come to save. As the war turned south the Americans became more frustrated and amped up the use of firepower. Bring on the B-52's! Ultimately the tonnage dropped by strategic air in Vietnam tripled that of WWII. The only real concern we had in Korea was if the war got any larger where would that leave us? The National Guard in the United States was not going to be tapped for manpower. These fortunate sons had the golden ticket that prevented them from participating in the carnage. Had the George W. Bushes and Dick Cheneys been called upon to enter the fray, the war would have been concluded much earlier.

Fortunately, a gentleman named Clark Clifford saw that the light at the end of the tunnel could only be seen by those who wished to see it. The decision was made to de-escalate. The strategic errors made during the Vietnam War are now receding into history. Those that lived the experience are now senior citizens. A lesson that should have been learned but was not is that there has to be a viable political force in a nation at war. The Communists in the North referred to the South Vietnamese government as "Puppets". The obvious conclusion drawn is that once the Americans leave the "Puppets Fall". Before the disastrous war in Iraq was fought the politics or lack thereof should have been closely examined. The Bush administration did not even consider or know about the schism in Islam. The Sunnis and Shiites disliked each other intensely, and the Iraqis were simultaneously fighting the Americans and each other. Introspection is not the strong suit of Americans. The subsequent fighting in Fallujah is illustrative of this. The locals were the "insurgents" and the Americans were the good guys. After we left, the country dissolved into chaos. Has the fourth estate reported on this fiasco? The answer is no. The same pundits who reported on the justness of our cause and the fact that the Iraqi people would greet us with flowers are still at it. Did they suffer any damage to their careers? Any loss of credibility? Far from it, the experts are unassailable. Fox news is still considered to be a legitimate information source by the other networks. Critical thinking is for liberals.

The architects of our disastrous foreign policy decisions of the last decade are now featured speakers in commencement ceremonies at ivy league schools. In contemporary America nothing succeeds like failure. George W. Bush "you are either with us or the terrorists" is now immortalizing himself on canvas. Winston Churchill, move over!

Chapter 8

The fate of the Pueblo crew was still uncertain. We were going on alerts more frequently as autumn approached. The North Koreans were making all sorts of demands. Saving or preserving face is very important in the orient. It is very difficult for the occident to understand the cultural imperative of honor. A container ship bound for America from Japan with hundreds of new sub-compact automobiles experienced serious flooding in one of the cargo bays. Sea water had entered the hold and a portion of the autos were destroyed. The captain observed the damage, returned to his cabin and cut his throat. He did not wish to face a court of inquiry. The deceased and his family were accorded the highest honors by the government, and he received what amounted to a state funeral. An American ship captain would hire a lawyer and plead the Fifth Amendment. There is much to be admired in Japanese culture.

The entire Pueblo incident has mystified me over these many years. I had the opportunity to talk to several of the crew in the 642 hospital before they were spirited off to America for de-briefing. The Navy was apparently unaware that communist infiltrators were landing on the east coast of Korea and attempting to subvert the government of Park Chung Hee. We had our own sophisticated electronic spying of the north on going. Why did the Navy send an unarmed cargo ship into North Korean territorial waters to do the same thing? What I have been able to deduce is the Navy was unaware of the Army electronic surveillance of the North and vice-versa. Much the same scenario was evident in the intelligence failure of 9/11. The CIA was not sharing information with the FBI. In any event the resulting capture of the AK Pueblo and its crew of 83 men was a major embarrassment to the United States.

Shortly after Ronald Reagan moved into the White House in January 1981, Nancy Reagan had an informal press conference. She said something that remains vivid in my mind, "It's hard to live on $200,000 dollars a year." My heart went out to her on the great sacrifice of serving the country on such a paltry salary. When they say there's no business like show business I think I know why. Poverty is a relative thing. Most Americans in 1981 would have been euphoric at the thought of such a princely sum, but not Nancy. Asian poverty would have caused her to swoon. Many of the families that ran grocery stores in Bupyong lived, worked and died in their places of business. I occasionally purchased Raman Noodles which I cooked over the space heater in our barrack. One evening I stopped in the store just before closing. The mama-san was spreading out the mats for the night and the children were putting on heavy clothing in preparation for bed. They were sleeping directly behind the counter of the establishment on the floor. Counting the children there were four living in one twelve by fourteen foot room. How cold it may have gotten in that small cubicle at night, I do not know.

The stores in Bupyong at that time sold an interesting array of products. One establishment dealt in herbal and snake medicines. There was an entire shelf of snakes cut up in two to three inch sections. They were pickled and placed in mason jars for the potential customers to view. I asked a bilingual Korean what they were for, "Everything," he explained. Rheumatism, impotency, indigestion, headaches, you name it. The manager would select the appropriate snake for the specific malady. The mysteries of the orient puzzled this occident. Acupuncture was also practiced at several establishments in town. At the time western physicians pooh-poohed the practice, but later empirical evidence proved it worked. Years later, I saw on television, a Chinese woman wide-awake delivering a baby by Caesarian section without the aid of anesthesia. The only visible aids to reduce pain were numerous needles placed in her abdomen.

About this time an incident at Panmunjom occurred that

made the front page of the Pacific Stars and Stripes. Tensions were high regarding the still imprisoned Pueblo crew. The U.S. and ROK armies were providing security during the negotiations. It was unusual for Americans and North Koreans to come anywhere near each other but on this day they did. The innocent American GI offered his North Korean counterpart a stick of gum, his reward was a hard kick in the testicles. An American lieutenant immediately tackled the North Korean and began pummeling him. Why this incident did not start a second war, I do not know. A North Korean officer ran out and pulled his now bloody subordinate from under the American officer and said something in English. Both sides backed off. Cooler heads prevailed and a formal complaint was lodged through the UN command. The poor GI wound up in our hospital, part of his right testicle was surgically removed. What happened next could have resulted in hostilities. Starlight telescopic sights were mounted on M-14 rifles which gave Americans control of the night. I have no absolute proof that this shooting happened, but I heard it from two sources years later. The kicking incident became well known among the GIs in the 2nd and 7th Infantry divisions. They wanted retribution. One night a week or two later, a North Korean soldier was in the DMZ looking around. An alert American infantryman spotted him through his night vision scope and followed him. He may have been burying mines or looking for them. He appeared to be unarmed, very unusual. Possibly he was part of a patrol. He stopped mid-stride lowered his pants and squatted. A shot rang out and the DPRK soldier toppled to the ground. Score one for Uncle Sam. Now the North Koreans had a score to settle with us. The not uncommon method of getting even was placing mines on the American side of the MDL or military demarcation line. The Communists had a devilish contrivance made out of plastic. This mine was virtually undetectable with a conventional mine detector. It was small about the size of a twelve gauge shotgun shell. If you stepped on it with the front of your boot you lost your toes. If your heel hit first you lost your leg. Considering most ambush patrols were mounted at night, it was a risky proposition to trod the DMZ.

Apparently the Communists decided to up the ante. One dark night the sound of diesel engines was heard, many diesel engines also the distinctive clanking of tank treads. Starlight scopes revealed the movements of at least a regiment of armored vehicles. This apparently was some sort of a show of force. It is difficult to describe what total darkness is to Westerners. There is ambient light virtually everywhere in America, even in rural areas. The only experience I have had in civilian life to rival the darkness in Korea was Yellowstone National Park in September. The infantrymen along the DMZ had never experienced anything to rival the racket they heard that September night. By agreement, no weapon heavier than a machine-gun or mortar was permitted north of the Imjin River. There was division artillery but it was miles away down south. A Lieutenant got on a PRC-25 radio and requested an illumination round. The battalion answered in the negative, "We cannot authorize the use of illumination without approval from regiment." Regiment was contacted, "We cannot authorize the use of illumination without approval from division." Division was contacted, "We cannot authorize the use of illumination without the approval of corps." I do not think that President Johnson was in on this, but somewhere along the chain of command permission was granted. One round from a 105 howitzer some miles away was fired. Flares fired from a howitzer are attached to parachutes and they stay up a long time. This must have shaken up the North Korean tank commanders, they may have expected an artillery concentration to follow. Motors were gunned and they headed north rapidly. End of story. The game of chicken continued.

About this time I made the acquaintance of a Swedish Colonel named Lars Svenson. The Colonel was part of the United Nations command and delivered a monthly diplomatic pouch to Pyongyang. He was the only individual I ever met who had traveled north of the 38th parallel. He was obviously very intelligent because he spoke flawless English. The Colonel suffered from eczema and was using a medication only available

At the 642. I cannot remember exactly how we got into a discussion but the question arose, "What was life like in North Korea?" The Colonel stated, "Pyongyang is a modern capital with broad streets and modern buildings, but no vehicles or pedestrians. I have never seen what appears on the surface to be normal city without people." I asked what it was like to deal with the Communists. He answered that they say as little as possible and are very suspicious of Westerners. We are met at Panmunjom by the military, escorted to the capital and put up in a government hotel for the night." He further stated, "What few civilians we see will not look at us. They are afraid of their own army." I never saw the Colonel again. I admired him for his courage.

The North Koreans had their own English speaking Tokyo Rose. She was called Pyongyang Polly. Polly could speak good English and between insults to the "American Gangsters" and the "South Korean Running Dogs", she played American songs. I guess they liked "Home on the Range" because they played it all the time. An officer in the unit had a short wave radio, and was able to pick up Russian broadcasts from Siberia. There was apparently some sort of border dispute between the Russians and the Chinese. I found out years later that there were shootings and some deaths along the Yussouri River. So much for "Communist Solidarity". The Army station was called Radio Tomahawk after the shoulder patch of the 2nd Infantry division. The morning broadcast was followed by the instrumental from "We've got to get out of this place" by the Animals. The powers that be never caught on.

I occasionally worked the day shift at the hospital which I did not like. There were constant inspections and administrative officers looking for something to complain about. Second or third shift was the best; just two people, one nurse and one medic. The nurses normally kept the records and the medics did the nursing. Passing medications was about the only time they got off their gluteus maximus and walked around. One nurse actually said, "Don't get the idea that you are running things around here private!" I wanted to say, "If you would get off your dead ass the patients might become familiar with you!" Fortunately for me, silence was golden.

Many patients were curious about the nature of their illness. One day a young GI came in the ward with a diagnosis of sarcodosis. I already had a nodding familiarity with this condition and realized it was serious. He asked me if I could supply him with more information, "No problem" I said. I went to the medical library and removed the appropriate book and gave it to him. I got back to the patient about an hour later and he appeared very distraught and fearful. He had read about the condition and panicked.

The next day the attending physician confronted me and he was visibly agitated. When he asked to see me in private I knew I had committed a major faux pas. He stated "Sirkin, you have no authority to remove medical books from the library and share information with patients. There are varying degrees of severity with sarcoidosis. He has the mild form. You have succeeded in frightening the daylights out of this young man, and I hold you personally responsible." I gulped hard, and prepared to receive some sort of punishment. "Never do anything like this again, do you understand?"

"Yes Sir," I replied. He never reported the incident. There was a similar situation several weeks later. A Sergeant was admitted with a hacking cough. I bundled his uniform up and placed it in storage. I returned to the ward and checked his file: fulminating carcinoma bi-lateral. This life-long smoker was doomed. I talked to him and asked him if he was aware that he was to be evacuated. He said, "Yeah, they want to drain my lung. Once that is done, I'll be O.K." This time I kept my mouth shut. The penchant for not sharing information with patients puzzled me at the time. I suppose it prevented panic in some patients but just delayed the inevitable. The nurses would not tell the patients what medications were being administered. Possibly they figured the GIs were incapable of understanding basic pharmacology.

One evening I left the ward on break and walked up to the helipad to have a quick cigarette. It was past dusk with limited visibility. I saw a physician with a headlock on one of the village whores dragging her to his quarters. She was flailing around a little but appeared to be about to surrender to his demands. Normally business was done without any problems. Cash on the barrel head was sufficient to gain cooperation. What had precipitated this confrontation was a mystery. Possibly he had some other activity in mind than standard intercourse. Many of the bar girls would not perform blow-jobs. However, if the price was right, some would do practically anything. Cyrus Vance came to South Korea in February 1968 to discuss the deteriorating situation with North Korea. He stayed at the Presidential residence The Blue House. A detail of the 728 MP Company was tasked with guarding him. About 11:00 P.M. three beautiful Korean women entered his quarters. The lights went out. They did not emerge until 6:00 A.M. the next day. The MP's laughed like hell afterward. I have no idea how much rest the envoy got. Foreign aid goes both ways.

A number of the 642 nurses were engaged or married to officers serving in Vietnam. I needed some ace bandages one day and went to a neighboring ward to borrow some. Lt. Lewis was reading a letter from her fiancé in Vietnam. He was a Warrant Officer Huey pilot ferrying combat troops around Cu Chi. I asked her how he was doing and she stated there was a great deal of fighting going on but he hoped to make the Army a career. I said, "When and if the war ends, there won't be much need for helicopter pilots." She brushed off my statement and I went about my work. About six weeks later I learned that her boyfriend had been killed in action. I went to see her and offered my sympathy. Her reddened eyes indicated that she had been crying for some time. Several weeks later I learned that she had taken up connubial relations with a newly arrived male nurse. Mourning periods in those days were very brief. One evening on break I walked down to the mess hall for a snack. The cooks were very good about leaving fruit and cereal for the night shift. Sp/4 Miller motioned me over to a table and I sat down. "Take a look at what we confiscated from a new admission to the psych ward". A psychological profile had arrived from Vietnam with his souvenir photo collection. Two pictures were memorable, one was of a beheaded Vietcong with a cigarette sticking out of his mouth propped up on a tree branch. A smiling GI stood nearby pointing at the head. The second was of a Vietnamese about two feet off the ground stuck to a tree with his arm across his chest. I inquired, "What the hell is this?" The corpse appeared to be nailed to the tree.

"Beehive artillery round", came the reply.

"What is a beehive artillery round?" Turns out that it is a flechette filled 105 mm artillery projectile that was developed during the Korean war to prevent artillery batteries from being overrun by the Chinese. It acts like a giant shotgun that sweeps everything before it with thousands of nail like projectiles. "I never heard of it," I said.

Miller replied, "Heard about it from some artillerymen that came through the hospital. They have them up north."

Apparently these photos were immediately destroyed. Only three or four people saw them. Several nights later I went to the ville' for a few drinks. I looked up Yobo and she seemed to be glad to see me. We went for a walk in the dark and wound up on a dike surrounding a local rice paddy. I was never much of a drinker, several beers were sufficient to make me lose my equilibrium. It was very dark and I fell off the dike into the feces filled rice paddy. Yobo dissolved in laughter she clapped her hands and yelled, "Sheep Palomar" Korean for "fucked up". I crawled out of the paddy covered in mud and she threw her arms around me and gave me a kiss. Apparently she thought my stupidity was worthy of reward. "You so funny," she said. "You come see me tomorrow. I cook for you." I never understood women.

Summers were the worst for infiltration. In the winter "line crossers" were easy to track in the snow. The infantrymen on the DMZ could relax a little. I never quite understood why these DPRK commando teams thought they could start some type of popular uprising among their southern cousins. Communism was hated and feared among the southerners. I knew there was a serious problem because every off duty ROK soldier was armed. They carried a mixed bag of weapons M-1 Garands, carbines, and .45 caliber grease guns. There was also a nightly curfew. Nothing in the village moved after 11:00 P.M. and anyone who was walking about after that hour, was subject to questioning by the National Police.

I hadn't seen much of Tom Grimaldi in weeks. He had a steady girlfriend in the village and spent most of his off duty time with her. I saw him walking down a corridor in early September and said hello. He looked very pale so I asked him what was wrong. He said, "They just brought in the body of a North Korean soldier shot in the DMZ"

"Why did they do that, if he is dead?"

"It's what they did to him after he was shot," replied Tom.

"What happened?"

"Some Seventh Division infantrymen tied him to the back of an APC and dragged him along the ground for a distance before they stopped. All the flesh is gone from his back. You can see his spinal column."

"What are they going to do?"

"Who knows?" came the reply. "There is probably going to be an investigation." There was no investigation, the body was removed and nothing further happened.

****

Yobo cooked the meal and it was very tasty. Afterward we repaired to her room and proceeded to make love. Yobo liked to fuck. She would turn bright red and begin to perspire heavily. Her eyes were always closed. Afterward she would immediately go to sleep. She never asked me for money. Try as I might it was impossible for me to break it off. I asked her once why she didn't try some other line of work. She would say, "I lazy. No education." She was smart, no doubt about it. Her knowledge of English was far superior to most of the other painted ladies. In any event my visits were very infrequent.

****

Toward autumn, the crew of the Pueblo was making propaganda broadcasts for the North Koreans, one of the more memorable was transcribed by Army intelligence. It ran about like this: "The U.S.S. Pueblo was prepared with unmitigated acidity and rank boldness to be a clever diabolical scheme to strike terror into the palpitating breast of the People's of the DPRK. Only the finest possible ship was selected to carry its super-spy trained crew. Upon reporting to the Pueblo on duty, I found out I was to be first indoctrinated by the most notorious super-spy within the seething inwards of the navy. I was to be trained by none other than Commander Buzz Sawyer. He immediately commenced a rigorous training program, which was designed to teach me the finer points of provocation and nastiness." Commander Bucher was taking a real risk in committing this material to paper. If someone in the West were to read such doggerel and it got back to the North Koreans that he was making fools of them, there would be hell to pay. It turned out later they did pay a significant price.

The barracks assignments were changed. Just when you got to know a group of people the coffee-klatch was broken up. Billet assignments were made on the basis of which unit you were assigned to: internal medicine, surgical, post-operative, or orthopedic wards. Since I spent most of my time in internal medicine, off I went to my new quarters. The two new barrack NCO's I will refer to as Sturm and Drang. Both were SFCs and lusted after that third rocker. Sturm was a neatness freak, a place for everything and everything in its place. I kept reading material in a box under my bed. Most of the troops, if they read at all, consumed so called "fuck" books. The more lurid, the better.   I read some Hemmingway, Mark Twain, and history. The Army, to its great credit, did not discourage reading, but saw to it that the library was well stocked. Even Masters and Johnson had a place as noted earlier. Sgt. Sturm was not a reader and a cardboard box under a bed was not in the regulations. He simply picked up the material and tossed it out the back door. Sgt. Jones, whom I mentioned earlier in connection with the homosexual affair saw my name on the box and placed it under his bed. As an NCO, he had a cubicle with a door. I never forgot this act of kindness. He was a tough inner-city black from Detroit but cut me more slack than I deserved. He was a fine man with a sense of humor who was also something of a legend for his actions in Vietnam. The senior NCOs seemed to view the draftees as threats to their chances for promotion. We were constantly creating problems for them and were viewed as untidy, disrespectful, malcontents who cooperated reluctantly. Sturm and Drang had some positive traits, at least they were not heavy drinkers. I seldom saw them except at bed time.

There were rumblings that some major changes were in the offing. Four staff were leaving the 642. They were headed for the only other evacuation hospital in Korea located in Pusan. The reason for these changes soon became apparent. Walter Reed in Washington was transferring the team that cared for former President Eisenhower to Korea. They were given the choice of Vietnam or Korea. The safer option was taken. President Eisenhower, it turned out, was experiencing congestive heart failure. His major heart attack in 1955 was followed by minor strokes that had impaired his speech. The new team was quite open about discussing his deteriorating condition. These nurses and medics soon became aware that Korea was not Washington D.C. There were no amenities whatsoever. They did not express any real discomfort publically but the expressions on their faces showed their dissatisfaction. A new SSgt arrived on the scene about this time. He wore a nylon cap on his head. I puzzled about this. The story was that SSgt. Orin Blaylock was scalped in Vietnam, not by the Vietcong rather an APC. As the story went, his armored cavalry unit came under mortar attack. Blaylock hugged the armored personnel carrier a bit too closely. It lurched forward knocking off his helmet and caught his hair in the tracks The top of his scalp was torn off. He was undergoing plastic surgery which was no simple process. Had the track reversed course rather than moving forward he would have been crushed to death.

Chapter 9

I graduated from the University of Illinois in 1971. My first teaching job was in a modestly gentrified community on the south side of Chicago. It was a changing community, by that I mean minorities were moving into the area and the locals were not happy. The Army left me with an egalitarian feeling towards my fellow men. I had good relations with all my students and quickly squelched any inappropriate comments from them. The teachers on the other hand were not on a par with the students. There was a pecking order. The physics teachers held themselves above the biology teachers. Life sciences were held below the 'hard sciences'. The principal had frequent parties at his home trying to foster harmony among the staff. One of the history teachers was a Princeton graduate. His friend was a Brandeis grad and a teacher of English. These two gentlemen viewed themselves as the sharpest tools in the box and looked upon yours truly, a former college drop-out, as a loser. Mr. Steinway was regaling the teachers about his prowess at "Jeopardy" which was and remains one of the most popular question and answer shows on television. He stated, "I can beat anyone at this party, hands down, at Jeopardy." This braggadocio was beginning to grate on me. Steinway was referring to my wife as "Butch." I figured if I got up and took a swing at the S.O.B. my teaching career would be over before it started so I cleared my throat and said, "Steinway, I will beat you and your Princeton pal at Jeopardy even if you combine your scores!" We jumped in our autos and repaired to the home of the French teacher. Out came the Jeopardy board and we did battle from about 11:30 P.M. to 2:00 A.M. I was beating these two worthy gentlemen so badly that the French teacher was doing her best to lip sync the correct questions. In the end we played three complete rounds. I mastered them on two out of three, they won the third barely. My scores exceeded their combined totals. These two characters lost by a not-insignificant margin. Did this gain me entry into the inner circle? Was I recognized as the college-drop-out savant? I was more marginalized than ever. They could never accept the fact that I knew more than they did. The Princeton Grad was trying to get into law school, but he was rejected. The people in the English department prided themselves on their ability to turn a phrase. Quarterly, we had to send progress reports home to the parents to apprise them of their children's progress. The principal was proud of some of the comments and printed many of the better ones as an inspiration to those of us who lacked creativity. One memorable example, "Judith thinks her physical presence in class is sufficient recompense for her lack of effort." Recompense! I had to laugh. This florid rhetoric had not been used since Othello slew Desdemona! Was it supposed to inspire us? After two years, I quit. Apparently, I was from the wrong socio-economic group to gain any traction with these patricians. I was asked once why I had started my teaching career at such an advanced age. I told them I had spent time in the Army. You would have thought my name was Joseph Mengele! This was not a career booster in 1973, so I moved on.

****

My second job as a public school teacher was at Madison Junior High in Oak Forest, Illinois. Madison served a working class neighborhood in a residential community just outside of Chicago. I taught physical science: six classes per day. The program was laboratory-based and followed a hands-on basic science curriculum, I thought the program was an excellent one and pitched in with enthusiasm. It soon became obvious that there was palpable tension between the staff and the principal. I did not understand why for several months. The secretary, as most school secretaries, did a good deal of work to keep things humming. Ruth was amazing, she bandaged injured fingers, wrote out daily attendance reports, collated grades for each of the four hundred plus students, kept health forms tidy and up to date, practically everything. One day I arrived early and found Ruth busily engaged in brewing coffee. I asked, "Why are you here so early Ruth?"

"The principal likes his coffee when he comes in." She replied.

"Is this part of your job description?" I intoned. She just chuckled. One of the English teachers also liked his coffee in the morning. Mr. Clark was a single man who prepared strong coffee for himself and several others. He thoughtfully offered me a cup one day, and I became a regular recipient. The principal became aware of this custom and said it had to stop due to the fact that hot coffee carried through the halls posed a threat to the students. Since few students were present in the halls at 7:30 A.M. I thought this rule was silly and arbitrary. Mr. Clark ignored the order and the coffee was proffered each day. He was a nice man. Several months later I came in early and stopped by the office for my mail. It was not yet 8:00 A.M, Ruth was busily typing away at the IBM Selectric. I said, "My, you are really dedicated, starting so early."

She turned to me and said, "Mr. White said he wanted this done by 3:00 P.M. today."

"What's the rush?" I asked.

"The Principal's brother-in-law has a job interview tomorrow and needs an updated resume."

"You are typing personal correspondence for Mr. White?"

"That's right," she replied.

"Why don't you complain?"

"They would fire me."

I began to get an inkling of what was to come. Mr. White put himself above the students and faculty; apparently his personal business took priority over school matters. At the end of my first year the graduation exercises were presided over by the Principal. He stood up and proudly stated, "The product we generate at this school is on a par with any other Junior High in Northern Illinois." I was somewhat taken aback, "product?" The students were now on a par with newly manufactured bicycles, or toasters? It became clear at this early date that the corporate model was now being used as a yardstick for progress in education.

Year two was met by yet another example of how our principal dealt with problem students. Mr. Peregrin was an elderly English teacher. He was well liked by the faculty, and respected by the students. One particularly troublesome pupil would not follow directions and do his work. Peregrin seldom removed students from class. This particular day he left his room and deposited the misbehaving kid in the school office which was located immediately next to my room. Less than five minutes later, I observed the principal returning with the trouble-maker to Mr. Peregrin's class. I sought him out after school and asked, "Jim, did the principal make any effort to discipline your student, or contact the family?"

He looked up at me and answered, "White refuses to get involved with discipline, he always says the same thing: it is the teacher's responsibility to contact the parent."

"How about an after school detention, or having the misbehaving students sweep the floor?"

Jim just laughed, "White beats the teachers to his car. He is the first one out of the building."

"How can this be allowed to continue?"

Peregrin answered, "As long as the parents don't complain, the superintendent will not get involved." Most of the teachers refrained from criticism of the administration. They did not even talk among themselves and, as it turned out, some of my colleagues even informed on each other. Silence was golden. I decided to help. If Peregrin or any other teacher on the second floor had real difficulty with a student, they should send them to my science class. I would supervise for the remainder of the period. This informal system seemed to work. Since the principal only left his office between periods to monitor student movement, he never caught on. In the course of my thirty-three years of teaching I met many fine dedicated people. This administrator was the exception. I believe the motivation for his behavior was due to fear of compromising his job by offending a parent or forcing a confrontation with someone. Avoidance is a tactic.

By my fifth year at Madison I had learned that the less frequently I had dealings with the front office, the better. Returning to school in August of 1982, I was greeted by the aroma of liquid tar. I went to see Ruth but was unable to find her, I tried the faculty lounge, there she sat. "How long has this been going on?" I exclaimed.

"About a week," she responded.

"I learned that the estimate for the work was lower if the company was given the opportunity to complete it after the regular season."

"You mean to say that this is going to continue after the students arrive in three days?"

"That's right." she replied. "The smell is bad enough but the roof is leaking, they apply water at some point in the process."

I could not believe it. To save some money the school board had delayed the re-tarring of the roof to coincide with the beginning of the school year. "This is it as far as I am concerned, I want to talk to the principal, where is he?" Ruth smirked a little and said, "He hasn't been here for more than an hour all week. I am supposed to handle the new enrollments myself." Needless to say, the beginning of the school year was terrible. The students complained constantly. Parents were up in arms, why wasn't the job done in June or July when the students were on summer break? Could the Superintendent and School Board be that contemptuous of the students, faculty, and community? The situation got worse in October.

All of the teachers at Madison were instructing six classes per day plus lunch room supervision. This left us with precisely twenty-five minutes to eat and relax each day. At the school board meeting in October, a delegation of faculty members, including me, showed up in an attempt to get some relief from lunch room supervision. A twenty-five minute lunch was insufficient to digest a meal and rest. The board members listened to our concerns for about twenty minutes and we waited for the chairman to reply. He cleared his throat and said, "If you don't like it here you can quit and get a real job." So this was it, we really weren't working. Teaching was not a profession. At this point I decided it was time to leave, but I still had seven months remaining in the school year. I had an unemployed wife and two children to worry about. I explained the situation to her and she suggested it was time to look for work. Being a qualified teacher she was willing to take up the burden if I was willing to care for the children. We both agreed to send out resumes as soon as possible.

The situation remained static until mid-April. About 1:30 in the afternoon I heard a student running down the hall, he reached the office and was immediately followed out of the door by the principal. I heard a siren approaching the school and realized there was a major problem. We had asthmatic students and I assumed that was the emergency. Two paramedics gained the top of the staircase, they approached Peregrin's room and disappeared inside. Several moments later Jim emerged from class and proceeded down the corridor with the paramedics in full pursuit. He descended the stairs and made it out to the ambulance under his own power. I had no idea what had happened but found out later in the day that a student had run to the office and told the secretary that the teacher was talking but was making no sense. His speech was slurred and he could not maintain equilibrium. Obvious signs of a stroke. After the day ended, I immediately went to the local hospital. Jim was sitting up in the emergency room and talking to a physician. I was told by several other teachers that had preceded me to the hospital, Jim had suffered a mild stroke. "Where is White?" I inquired.

"He never showed up." said the other teachers. This was it, the final straw! The son-of-a-bitch did not have enough concern for his own staff to see if one of them lived or died. Three weeks later Jim returned to school. He was observed by the principal in class at least twice a week for the next month.

I was now a thirty-eight year old father of two with no job and no prospects. My wife managed to obtain a teaching position and my mother agreed to watch our two children. This was no easy task as she was seventy-eight years old. I was a change of life baby and her only child. I decided to remain in teaching and to start substituting. I registered as a sub at the local high school. I could teach chemistry and biology with little difficulty and was called on a regular basis. The school secretary was as efficient as all the others and kept me at the top of her sub list. Fortune smiled on me. The long term chemistry teacher needed an operation for a hernia and I was asked to fill in. I said that high school chemistry was an area where I felt comfortable and would be more than willing to take up the task. I began on a Monday morning; the students looked at me askance and figured that I did not know anything. The class was already in the middle of Chapter Four and immediately the students began asking questions. I was able to work the factor label problems without much difficulty and after two or three days they accepted me. I went through the class rosters each day to familiarize myself with the student's names. The Hispanic pronunciations posed no difficulty and I began to get smiles from the kids. One young lady came to me after class and said, "Mr. Sirkin, you are the first teacher I ever had that pronounced my name correctly, thanks." Miss Padilla promptly asked to be moved closer to the front of the classroom.

About the second week of my substitution gig, the Department Chair dropped by my class and asked how things were going. I answered that it was fine. He simply said, "I haven't heard any complaints from the students about your work, thanks." About the third week, I inquired how much longer I could expect to sub for Mr. Dohrnberg. The department chair said, "I am sorry, I forgot to tell you. Mr. Dohrnberg has developed some post-operative problems and will be out for another week or two. Would you be willing to stay on?" I tried to conceal my delight. I was really enjoying myself and the students began to say hello to me between classes. After the forth week, Mr. Dohrnberg appeared to say hello to the staff and students and announce his imminent return. He walked into my class and the students greeted him warmly. One student told him that Mr. Sirkin had done a good job, he seems to know the material and never looks at the textbook.

A week later Dohrnberg returned. The principal dropped in my class and shook my hand. He said, "Mr. Blair told me you were the best science substitute teacher he ever saw. He wants you as a regular." I was very touched by these comments. Sure enough I began to get calls at least three times a week. I subbed in English, French, Mathematics, Special Education, you name it. The year flew by quickly and summer break marked the end of my academic year. No paycheck for three months.

I sent out numerous resumes and got no responses. In the middle of July, I received a phone call from the Department Chair at Garfield High. Mr. Blair asked me if I would interview for a maternity leave position that was available in the fall. "Would you be interested in teaching biology full time?" he said. I was very happy to be offered an opportunity and quickly acceded to his request .

The interview went very well. Principal Collins asked me how I would deal with a deeply religious student who believed in biblical creation vs. Darwinian evolution. I cleared my throat and said, "I can teach it either way." Both the department chair and the principal broke into loud laughter. I got the job.

Teaching in a good high school is as close to an ideal job as one can get. The students were bright and well motivated. There were virtually no discipline problems. After about three months the Department Chair approached me and asked me about my college transcript. Apparently, based on my performance as a substitute they had not examined it before I was hired. "We noticed that you dropped out of college in your junior year is that correct?" queried Mr. Blair.

"That is correct" I said. "I returned to the University of Illinois after I got out of the Army and completed my degree."

"It states here that you have a degree in Elementary Education."

"Yes Sir," I said. "I was a Chemistry Major before dropping out."

"OK," said Mr. Blair. I knew then it was not OK, there were plenty of Science Majors looking for full time work with excellent academic credentials and no black marks. I knew that at the end of the year would be the end of my time at Garfield. The year passed quickly. A biology proficiency test was administered in May of that year. Of the three biology teachers at Garfield, my students received the top scores and I did not have the honors classes. The attitude among my colleagues was they must have gotten the tests mixed up. There was no mistake. I was out anyway.

I was really feeling down in the dumps. Out again and from a school that had proven a delight. However, fortune smiled on me again. There was yet another semester opening in a high school twenty-five miles away. A Science teacher was taking a semester sabbatical and the Principal was casting about for a substitute and called some of his friends. Mr. Collins had recommended me! I thought it best to be above board in discussing my checkered academic career with the new boss, he waved me off stating, "You received the highest recommendation from the Department Chair and Principal at Garfield. If you want the job it's yours." Principal Hurlbut proved to be a man of his word. The students were a good deal tougher than the kids I encountered at Garfield, but there were no incidents or real problems The semester passed quickly.

I was getting desperate, it was January 1984; cold and depressing. I was making weekly trips to the unemployment office and checking the help wanted ads in the local newspaper. One Sunday, I spied a small ad in the classifieds. It stated: "Wanted: Chemistry, Biology teacher needed immediately. contact Sr. Wendy, St. Patrick High School." It was another long drive but I replied to the Ad. I gave Dohrnberg, Collins, and Hurlbut as references and was hired in three days. The pay was very modest but it was a job and much needed. The principal told me that the previous teacher had made advances toward several of the girls. Parents had complained and he had been terminated. She was very pleased with the fact that I was married with children. The only bad part was the lengthy commute. The students were very happy to have a new teacher and they smiled at me the first day. Apparently the previous instructor was not cutting it in the classroom. We got down to the business of classwork and things went smoothly. The laboratory was a pleasant surprise; vintage 1940's but well equipped and supplied with sufficient glassware and chemicals to complete the academic year. The months passed quickly and things went smoothly. At the end of the school year, the Principal inquired if I would like to return in the fall. It was a pleasant environment with little stress and my rapport with the students was excellent. I agreed to return, the only problem was pay. Salary was considerably less than half of what a beginning Public High School teacher would make. With few options open, I vowed to do my best and endure the long drive each day. The school was very progressive and Darwinian evolution was accepted by the Church. I had a good four years.

My wife received a job offer near Chicago in 1988. It was at a large high school with excellent pay and benefits. We decided to make a move. Her salary was more than sufficient to cover expenses for the four of us. I could look for another job in the city. Housing prices were a problem, I did not want to live in another apartment. We managed to get a reasonably good home in the suburbs. The selling point was a huge lot, two-thirds of an acre with twenty-two large maple trees. My wife entertained the idea of getting a PhD in her chosen field but paying the bills and raising two children precluded these plans.

After purchasing our new home, I had to set about looking for another job. I vowed to try to keep it if I could. The constant changes and getting to know new colleagues was very difficult. I began interviewing. Fortunately, my references were excellent but perspective employers were a bit put off by my frequent job changes. In the summer of 1988, I interviewed at a Catholic high school on the near north side of Chicago. The principal was very forthright in his presentation of the science program. He made it apparent that the students were challenging and my task would not be easy. I think my time in the Army served me well. I was used to dealing with tough customers and would brook no challenges to my authority. The first year a student actually challenged me to a "mano a mano"! I laughed in his face and said. "I wouldn't risk my front teeth on that one El Nino." The students erupted in laughter; we had a good time.

The principal supported my decisions in every instance. He was a dedicated man and was very concerned with the progress of his charges. I respected his dedication and professionalism. My teaching colleague was a nun with many years of experience. We did not hit it off immediately. One day she came to me and complained about the condition of the Chemistry Lab. It had been a long day and I was tired. I said, "Alright already, keep your shirt on I'll get to it when I have time." Apparently my telling her, as a nun, to keep her shirt on, she found funny. That broke the ice. We had a great professional and personal relationship. She had a rare sense of humor and seemed to enjoy my company. Each year the guidance counselors came to me beaming with the latest ACT scores. They rose each year for the entire six years I remained at the school. Sister Nora and I were a good team.

As I look back on my life, these were the best years. I really felt I was accomplishing something in the company of teachers I admired and respected. In 1994 an opportunity opened up in a public high school in the suburbs. I interviewed for the position and got it. My salary approximately doubled. I took the position. I was reluctant to leave my friends, but with my children approaching college age I could not turn down the money. My learning curve included the following: a) increasingly, students were relying on electronic calculators to do math problems and without them they were virtually helpless; b) parental intercession in the child's education was lessening due to the pressures of work; c) socio-economic factors largely determined success in school.

Edison Senior High School was on the fringes of the inner city. The student population was predominately Hispanic. There were three thousand students enrolled in the school. What struck me, almost immediately, was the lack of communication between the teachers. There were very small gaggles of teachers that commiserated with each other in the lunch room, but that was about it. The shocking part about Edison was the gang activity. The police and guidance counselors identified at least twenty-two rival groups in the school. Police were always in attendance mornings and afternoons to prevent trouble. The primary difference between my previous place of employment and Edison was student motivation. Many, if not most of my students had parents who had not completed high school. The student's first language at home was Spanish. Teaching is never easy, but the barriers I encountered at Edison were overwhelming. It was very difficult to give homework assignments as sizeable percentages of the students simply would not complete any work. If it was not done in class, it simply was not finished. I realized the real reason for my hiring, I had worked in the inner city and the Principal and Department Chair reasoned I could survive in the extant environment. The female teachers seemed to avoid one colleague in particular. I found this to be strange until I learned the woman in question was hitting on the single ladies. One in particular was cornered by the afore mentioned person and groped. Sweet Jesus, what had I gotten myself into? To add insult to injury the upper level science teachers would not share equipment. I was told one storage room was off limits to teachers of freshman and sophomores. Science at any level is deadly dull if you do not perform experiments. I enjoyed doing laboratory work and so did the students. It was difficult for me to function without access to appropriate equipment and facilities.

About mid-year, achievement tests were administered to the kids. I came upon a new hire who was busily engaged in changing the answers on the test answer sheets. I was appalled.

This is one activity that I refused to participate in. My scores, when I received the results, were mediocre to poor. The lesson to be drawn from this experience was simple. If an achievement test or standardized exam is administered in schools to large numbers of students, the completed forms should be sealed and immediately sent to the testing center. Under no circumstances should teachers be allowed to score them or even examine them. The mania for high test scores has caused teachers to become fearful of losing their positions if they fail to measure up. The same criteria should be applied to Charter schools. One can assume that any test that is used to rate the performance of a teacher must not fall into their hands before grading. The fallacy of great teachers produce successful students is predicated on one myth. The vast majority of children of parents with poor to no education will never come close to the performance levels of suburban students whose parents are highly educated.

The root cause of poorly educated people is poverty. Poor people frequently cannot afford higher education. When I attended the University of Illinois in the late 1960's and early 70's, costs were modest. The Government and the States used to partially fund the Universities and local Junior Colleges which kept fees very low and affordable. Now, higher education has simply become a business and a highly profitable one at that. The spate of on-line universities and diploma mills keeps getting larger. When Charter Schools boast that 90% of their graduates go on to college, I would like to see the number of students who actually complete a baccalaureate degree. I had an experience several weeks ago that spoke volumes about the current craze for "Higher Education." I went to the local bank wearing a nylon jacket with the University of Illinois logo on it. The teller asked me if I was an alum. I answered in the affirmative. She said, "I graduated college with a degree in interior design, and a debt of $25,000 but this is the only job I could get." In microcosm, this is the essential flaw in everyone goes to college. The resultant costs do not guarantee a job in your field of study. Worse yet, the mania for higher test scores and more teacher accountability has spawned a potent political movement which states: the problem with American Education is the teachers! They are over-paid, under-worked, and given huge retirement packages. No one ever points out that free public education built America. The past is no longer prologue; it is bunk.

I was beginning to have second thoughts about my decision to leave parochial education and move back to a public school. The extra money was great, but I felt that I was not very effective. I was considering resignation but the administration beat me. I was terminated. This turned out to be one of the best things that happened to me in my life.

****

My overseas tour turned out to be 397 days. I really wanted to part company with the Army. I was bored, stressed out, and homesick. Worst of all, my future looked bleak. Chances of getting back into college did not seem promising. One evening I sought out a nurse and asked for a Seconal capsule. She gave me some song and dance about not issuing barbiturates without a doctor's order. I knew that one capsule was not going to compromise her career and certainly it would not be missed. I started yelling at her and could not stop. I called her a "stupid bitch" and some other choice epithets and stomped off. Major Dickens somehow got into the act and the nurse unloaded the entire episode on him. A private reading off an officer is a court martial offense. The next day, I was told to report to the orderly room at 14:00 hours to see "The Man." Captain Sideburns was Regular Army and a strict by-the-book officer. I arrived at his office on time and entered. I noticed the 1st Sergeant was not present. My eyes fell on a thick sheaf of paper, my God! It looked like the first draft of War and Peace. Was this document all about me? Sideburns entered and placed his hand on the stack. "Private," he said, "You really hate senior enlisted men and officers don't you?" I said nothing. "You derive sadistic pleasure in belittling people behind their backs, don't you?" I was mute. He continued in this vein for a period of time, I was no longer listening. I snapped back to consciousness when he said, "What do you have to say for yourself?"

I said, "Sir, if you honestly believe the things you have just said, throw the book at me. I deserve it." Sideburns visibly flushed. He did not expect a response like that. He said, "Report to me tomorrow at 0900, that's all." I had a little less than twenty-four hours to contemplate my fate. I thought at the minimum I would get some jail time. I tossed and turned all night long.

In the morning I rose early and headed to the orderly room. I inquired, "Is Captain Sideburns in?"

"No!" came the reply from the company clerk. He shoved a single piece of paper across the desk toward me and said, "Sign this!" I could not believe it! A measly twenty-five dollar fine! A simple article 15! I was not even confined to barracks! No company punishment! Once again, I had been spared the ignominy of a court-martial. No other enlisted man would have gotten off with a slap on the wrist. I did not even pay the fine. I had an enlisted friend in the finance office who tore up the document. Yet another get out of jail free pass. Had I been in the North Korean Army, I probably would have faced a firing squad. I found out later that Major Dickens was furious with the decision. He had my ass in the proverbial sling and wanted retribution. I knew this was my last chance. Any further incidents would result in jail time. I made a vow to "straighten up and fly right".

About this time "Cool Hand Luke" appeared in the post theatre. Since I worked nights, I was unable to see it. A not so subtle change occurred in the 642 Hospital, I was being saluted by the junior enlisted men. Saluted! What the hell was going on? After seeing the movie a year later, I realized my army peers were looking upon me as a reincarnation of Paul Newman. The guy who almost got shot by attempting to climb the fence to freedom! "I'm shaking that bush, Boss!" In the mess hall, I was getting extra portions of food. People wanted to buy me a beer at the enlisted man's club. I had no idea, at the time, of what was going on. The harassment almost came to a stop. My name disappeared from the extra duty roster. I was a celebrity. In Vietnam, as the story goes, "Cool Hand Luke" played for six weeks at the Long Binh theatre. When it was replaced by another film, the furor was such that it was brought back for another two weeks! Draftees could relate to old Luke. In 1988 I requested my DD-214 and Army records, about three months later I received an envelope with the documents and a Good Conduct Medal with my name on it. Someone at the Office of Awards and Decorations in Philadelphia had a sense of humor.

* * * * * * * * * * * * * * * *

My brief stint at Edison High School came to an end and I was once again out of a job. Fortunately, my career in Parochial Schools and as a permanent substitute guaranteed some good references so I started to send out resumes once again. I interviewed at several schools and the question arose, "Why so many different jobs?" I answered as best I could, but was viewed with suspicion. Finally, I got an offer. Again it was a near thing. A well-respected teacher had to resign in the middle of August due to the fact her husband was transferred by his company to New York State. The Principal needed a replacement fast and I was available. When I was hired, the Principal stated, "You come highly recommended, why did you leave your last school?"

I replied, "I was terminated due to poor academic scores."

"What sort of difficulty did you encounter?"

"I was unable to motivate the students and had difficulty relating to them."

She seemed satisfied with my answer. The year that followed was a joy. The students were from middle-class families and well-motivated. I spent about half of each week on lectures and half on laboratory work. I frequently departed from the text and answered any questions the students had on any subject. I was popular and had a good relationship with other faculty members. The years passed. One day a guidance counselor dropped by my room smiling broadly. "Mr. Sirkin" she said, "Many of the students I talk to want to major in Biology. What is your secret?"

"Make a class interesting and fun and the students will pursue the subject." Many of the teachers I met in the course of my career had matriculated from college and immediately began teaching. I had been around the block and had a wealth of experience to share with them.

Things were going well until the year 2000. I looked into the environmental records of the Presidential candidates and was appalled at the history of Bush and Chaney. Two former oil men elected to the highest offices in the land spelled bad news for the environment. I had already introduced the concept of climate change/global warming to the students several years before. Few other science teachers discussed it. Not part of the curriculum was the standard response. Habitat destruction was very much a part of biology and desertification of sub-Sahara Africa was an index of global warming and over-grazing. I mentioned both Republican Candidates and expressed my disapproval. Smart teachers should avoid politics at all costs, but I dove in.

Chapter 10

In 1976 there was an attack near Panmunjom that resulted in the deaths of several Americans. This episode was fortunately not the beginning of general hostilities, but illustrated the fact that the North Koreans could still engage in unprovoked attacks on Americans.

The Pueblo crew was still being detained by the North Koreans. We went on alert several times in August and September but nothing materialized. I seldom saw Yobo. It was too risky. Her periods of hostility were unpredictable. Casualties continued to come in from the DMZ, both Korean and American. Since I was no longer involved in the O.R. and seldom appeared on the extra duty roster, my interest in what was going on waned. One night a patient on my ward had a grand mal seizure. It was frightening to see. I attempted to get a pillow case in his mouth to prevent him from biting his tongue but was unsuccessful. He gasped and started to turn grey. I checked for a pulse and could not detect one. I jumped on top of the man and started CPR. Color began to appear in his face. I had never done this procedure before and was afraid I would break his ribs. Stopping briefly, I checked for a pulse, nothing. I continued for several minutes, suddenly he gasped and coughed. I felt for his carotid pulse, success! The floor nurse, Mrs. Kim, noticed what was going on and ran out of the ward looking for help and the crash cart. By the time she returned with the duty physician the man was breathing on his own. I checked his chart: malignant hypertension, complete kidney failure. There was no dialysis equipment available in Korea in 1968. He died about two weeks later. I realized at this point that the things I witnessed and participated in would never happen to me again, so I started to keep notes. My DEROS was March 1969 - still some time in the future.

"I FOUND A LOVE!" I was jarred out of my slumbers by soul music. 1:00 P.M in the afternoon. I had been asleep for less than five hours. A new man was assigned to my barrack. He loved his music, morning, noon and night. It was bad enough to be roused from one's sleep in the morning but whenever he returned from his shift on went the radio. I thought it might be a good idea to try days for awhile. It was not easy to change the schedule. Most medics did not want to work evenings or nights. I managed to get first shift after several weeks trying: seven to three. One morning, I arrived early and was summoned to the Dermatology clinic. The regular sergeant was off for the week. Dr. Lowenstein had a number of men waiting for treatment. I grabbed the clipboard and began calling the patients in. The first soldier was an African-American Sp/ 4 who had facial hair that had grown inward. With a set of tweezers I carefully began to pull the hairs out of his skin: this condition was only evident in blacks. It took some time to complete the task. The second patient was a Thai soldier; he had a peculiar lesion growing just below his lip. The physician asked me to take a swab and scrape the lesion and place the cotton in a screw top test tube. He said, "Sirkin, do you know how to use a 35mm camera?" I replied in the affirmative. I took several color photos of his face The Doctor told the Sergeant to wait outside. He shot me a look and said in a hushed voice, "I believe it is leprosy. Write out an order and have him placed in isolation pending the lab report".

The next day a military chaplain showed up. The Major was a regular Army type and looked more like an infantry officer, than a priest. He was a red faced Irishman who complained of a persistent rash on his neck. The Doctor examined it carefully and stated, "Major, you have basal cell carcinoma, the private will write out an evacuation tag, you will be going back to the States for treatment."

Amazingly, he did not want to leave. "Can't the condition be treated here?"

"Not advisable," stated Lowenstein. "Do you spend a

great deal of time in the field with the troops?"

"Yes," replied the chaplain.

"You have a very fair complexion and long term exposure to the sun particularly for red heads is inadvisable." The Major assented to the decision and returned to Camp Casey to prepare for departure. Lowenstein was a very impressive man. His diagnoses were mostly spot on. The dermatology clinic did pro bono work on Korean civilians. Most of the patients were women who had gotten small pox as children. Under the Japanese occupation there was no immunization program in effect as we know it in the West. The ladies were mostly in their mid to late twenties and terribly scarred. The derm-abrasion process ground off the epidermis in an attempt to get rid of the worst pock marks. The abrasive wheels used by the physician turned the face into a red mask. The women were mute during the entire procedure. They sat with their hands folded and eyes closed. It must have hurt terribly but they never uttered a sound. The doctor would come in weekends to perform this free service, there was a long waiting list.

Profiles were constantly arriving in Korea from Vietnam. Some of them should have been given medical discharges or sent to the States. One memorable case was a young Sp/4 who came into the clinic with the most hang-dog look I have ever seen on a human being. I asked him what the problem was. He said, "It is my penis." I ushered him into the Doctor's office and Lowenstein proceeded to ask him some routine questions. He finally pulled down his fatigue trousers and we beheld the problem. His penis was split lengthwise down the middle and yellow pus oozed from the wound. This was the worst thing I ever beheld in my life before or since. The Doctor looked on in disbelief. He said, "Private get the camera and photograph this! Also get an evacuation tag and fill it out." The soldier was checked into the hospital temporarily and gone in three days. There was a rumor in the army that a secret medical facility existed in the Philippines where GIs were sent who had incurable venereal diseases acquired in Vietnam. I do not know whether these rumors were true or false but this poor soldier qualified.

It was very difficult for Americans to understand Korean culture. Often, KATUSAs held hands when they walked around the base. This practice is taken as a sign of friendship in the Orient. The unschooled Americans took it as evidence of homosexual behavior. Its practice resulted in several unfortunate confrontations. I was not witness to the altercation, but one ignorant GI tossed a boot at one of the KATUSAs and called him a dirty queer. The Korean soldier proceeded to practice Tae Kwan Do on the GI. Fortunately there were other soldiers in the barrack who interceded to stop the fight. No program existed overseas to inform Americans of some of the basic customs practiced in the Orient. Apparently, no lessons in this regard were learned by the generals. I was amazed to see five years into the Iraq war that American soldiers were still screaming in English at Iraqis basic orders they should have learned in AIT. In WWII GIs were taught some fundamental German to communicate with the enemy: Hande Hoch! (Hands Up!); Waffen Nederlegen! (Drop your weapons!). Possibly the Army brass just did not care.

I learned from some surgical technicians that the head floor nurse Major Treadwell had breast cancer and was going to have a radical mastectomy. The procedure was carried out in such a manner that no enlisted man would get within fifty feet of the operating room. Apparently the hospital commander thought it inappropriate for lowly GIs to view the breast of an officer. I was very surprised that she was not air evacuated to the States. Within a week she was back on the job.

One day, Tom Grimaldi approached me and asked if I would accompany him and a group of other OR Techs on a sight-seeing tour to Seoul. I had the Saturday off and quickly agreed. There was a daily bus that made the journey to Youngsan. It was about a forty minute trip to this main Army base. The PX was large and you could get good quality hamburgers for $ .50. Nam Dae Moon is the old Imperial Gate in Seoul. Its importance is equivalent to the Eifel Tower in Paris. I had only been to Seoul once before, when Yobo and I caught the train to her family home. We went to the Secret Garden and a beautiful park on a tall hill overlooking central Seoul. The scent of pine and the well-tended plants were very beautiful. In the afternoon we were walking down a street viewing Sony electronics, and Nikon cameras when we were accosted by a smiling man who was overflowing with good will. This gentleman was delighted to greet the gallant Americans who rescued his country from evil communism. Would we join him for a late lunch? Why we were delighted! "Hands across the sea", so to speak. We followed him for several blocks and entered a small restaurant. We dined on bulgogi beef, rice with soy sauce, shrimp, everything. After the meal our host offered to supply us with female companionship. I began to smell trouble. When we politely declined his offer the waitress appeared with the bill. $137, not won but U.S. greenbacks! This may not sound like much today, but in 1968 it represented a month's pay to a soldier. We argued with the gentleman for some time to no avail. He finally said the police would be summoned if we failed to pay up. He concluded his remarks by saying, "We Koreans just as good as you Americans!" In this case, considerably better. I no longer remember how we came up with the money; it did not quite reach the $137, but was close enough to satisfy this hustler. Considerably chastened by the experience, we walked back to Youngsan and waited for the bus. In the aggregate we were all broke until the end of the month. I wrote my mother asking for $50. She sent me a check.

Not all of our adventures ended on a sour note. There was a beautiful beach near Inchon. In late summer a number of us made the journey. Venders on the beach sold delicious fried shrimp at bargain basement prices. I never had better seafood than I enjoyed in Korea. There was a raft floating out in an estuary of the yellow sea. Another medic I barely knew said, "Let's swim out to it." We asked several other soldiers who had joined the party if they were interested in making for the raft. They all said no. So it was just the two of us. We bounded into the water like two sea nymphs. About fifty yards out, I felt I was sliding sideways. I had never experienced anything like this in my Uncle's quarry. On we went, now well aware of the hidden current that was pulling us away from the raft. I struggled on but the raft did not appear to be getting any closer. My partner in this folly shot me a look that told me we had better remain calm. We were making progress, albeit very slow progress. Finally we reached the raft. I was exhausted. I did not have the energy to hoist myself aboard the float. Clinging to the side of the raft I glanced back to see if my associate was near. He was about seventy-five feet away. After a few moments, I regained some strength and hoisted myself aboard. Frank finally arrived and I helped pull him aboard. We lay there like beached whales, completely spent. By this time a group of people Koreans and Americans were standing on the beach waving to us. I think they sensed our predicament. How long we rested on that float I no longer recall, but we knew that we had to swim back. It was now late afternoon and we eased ourselves back into the water and made for shore. When we got back to dry land, a Korean police officer had appeared and through an interpreter he stated that it was dangerous to swim in this place when the tide went out. People had drowned in the immediate area. Further explanations were unnecessary. We returned to the beach several times, but never went in the water again.

Inchon was the port that General McArthur decided to land the 1st Marine Division in 1950. The 7th U.S. Army division landed a day later and proceeded to take Seoul. There was evidence of the fighting all over. Buildings bore the scars of battle, bullet strikes and artillery craters were still visible, Ocean going ships from all over the world came in to drop off and pick up cargo. Hyundai at that time made super-tankers that were just coming into vogue. On my infrequent visits to Inchon I encountered Australians, British, Japanese, New Zealanders and Americans. The houses of ill-repute were numerous and served the sailors who made port. I walked into one of these establishments one afternoon and beheld the most unattractive collection of whores one could imagine. Painted lady would not be an adequate description of some of the babes I saw. Their profligate use of rouge made them look like obscene clowns from some sort of mad circus. I was drinking my beer when the madam approached me and said, "Would you like to talk to Cherry Girl?" I declined and left. Two of the ladies actually ran out of the club and followed me. I guess it was a slow business day. "Hey you, come back!" they said in unison. I easily outdistanced them and made good my escape.

The first President of Korea was Syngman Rhee (no relation to Michelle Rhee). He was a graduate of Harvard and an early advocate for Korean independence. Rhee was not averse to making a little money on the side. His personal project in Inchon was a sugar beet refinery that was apparently never completed. What the exact circumstances were behind the abandoned building I never ascertained. Suffice to say, graft in the Orient was simply a way to survive. Approximately two million Koreans died in the war, practically every Korean that worked for Uncle Sam had a father, mother, uncle, or sibling killed in the war. Starvation and exposure accounted for many lives. It was a terrible war little reported by the American press. There was a heroic statue of General McArthur overlooking Inchon harbor. The tides at Inchon and the Bay of Fundy in Nova Scotia are the highest in the world. At low tide one could look out over hundreds of yards of mud flats to the Yellow sea beyond. There were scores of starfish, clams, and seaweed left high and dry. I walked out on the flats one day to examine the creatures. My journey did not last long as I was immediately ankle deep in mud.

Several ROK soldiers were admitted to the 642 Evac with serious gunshot wounds. One was admitted to a ward post-op and began to hemorrhage. He arrested and a physician began to administer CPR. The soldier turned from pink to ashen in several minutes. A plywood board was introduced under him and Dr. Meirs vigorously continued with chest compressions. The patient made a few agonized gasps and died. The other Korean survived: victims of yet another North Korean ambush. This was all so familiar by now, another pointless attack, more deaths. What did Kim Il Sung hope to accomplish? I was reaching the point when I just wanted out. Was this going to escalate into another war? The volunteer army is now suffering the effects of repeated overseas tours. More soldiers are committing suicide in the Army and Marine Corps than are killed in Afghanistan. The stress on these men is intolerable. There should be a draft. Most of America's wars were fought by volunteers or draftees. A professional military is what our founding fathers warned against. It has now come to pass that the American Army which always operated at the margins of society is now completely isolated from main street America. What cannot be accomplished by the volunteers is now in the hands of "contractors", a euphemism for mercenaries. We are paying a terrible price for our ignorance.

****

September 14, 1968

Radio Tomahawk announced this morning that Major General Keith L. Ware was killed in Vietnam. General Ware had received the Medal of Honor while serving in the 3rd Infantry Division in France during WWII. He single handedly wiped out several German machine gun positions and led fewer than a dozen men in taking a heavily contested hill. He was a LTC at the time. This incident brought home to me the intensity of the Vietnam War. The gallant gentleman was observing a firefight from his command helicopter, and it was shot down. All aboard perished.

About this time the announcement came down that we would have a full field inspection in several weeks. Officers fear two things: Congressional Investigations, and Full Field Inspections. A poor rating on a general inspection can result in black marks against a commander. There is a saying in the Army if it moves - salute it, if it doesn't - paint it! Sure enough out came the paint cans. Renoir did not select the painting schemes for Army instillations. Most of the WWII barracks were yellow everything else was painted in pea green. The floor polishers were in constant use and everything began to gleam. Rafters were dusted off. Every fly speck was removed from the walls and windows. There were no idle hands. On the appointed day the members of the company not on duty lined up in front of the hospital in greens and awaited the inspection team. It is not a good idea to stand at rigid attention for more than ten minutes. The secret to not falling flat on your face is keeping the knee joint flexed a little. The inspection team did not arrive on time, but no one called, "Parade Rest!" We stood there like the Coldstream Guards awaiting the arrival of Her Majesty. Then it happened, a thin Sp/4 passed out. He did not drop like the proverbial sack of potatoes, rather fell like a newly cut ponderosa pine. He described a beautiful 90 degree arc and landed flat on his face with a loud twack. Did anyone break ranks to see if he was all right? Not a chance. He just lay there unattended. Finally the inspection party arrived. To everyone's amazement they were all officers wearing the crossed rifles of infantrymen! These people might have been proficient at inspecting rifles, but were clueless about hospitals. The inspection proceeded, several of the officers equipped with clipboards descended on the operating room and proceeded to comment on its state of "readiness". One enlisted technician was putting up thoracotomy packs. The instruments were thoroughly washed and placed on blue cloth wraps and covered prior to autoclaving in superheated steam. An infantry Captain asked, "Aren't you going to sterilize the instruments before you wrap them up?" This became a standing joke in the O.R. for weeks. The Captain apparently had no clue about the autoclave. "War is Hell," commented one of the physicians when he heard the story. The inspection team traveled to the wards and the duty nurses explained their jobs. They mostly asked the patients about the quality of food and when they expected to be released. Those of us not on duty, stood inspection outside the hospital. Our hair length once again was thoroughly scrutinized. I was marked down for worn shoes. Shoe replacement was a big deal in the Army. If your boots or low quarters were worn you had to DX them for repair or replacement. My single pair of oxfords were just about shot. I submitted them for replacement and several weeks later they returned "repaired". The soles and heels had been replaced but the toes stood up like something an elf would wear. I could barely get my feet inside and it hurt to walk. The cobbler needed some serious remediation. At this point I gave up and went to the PX to buy a new pair of oxfords. The fee was $ 35.00. How they came up with such an indecent price was beyond me, but I needed a pair of "regulation" low quarters. At this time the pay of a private E-2 was $71.00 per month. Two weeks pay down the drain! More letters to mother pleading for money. I got into the black market trade. We were paid in scrip or "funny money". Uncle Sam did not want U.S. greenbacks falling into the hands of the enemy in the event of invasion from the north so we were paid in orange dollars. No George Washington gazing down from a cloud, rather some broad with a shield and spear. The Koreans would accept scrip reluctantly, but preferred dollars. I purchased instant coffee from the PX and sold it to the Koreans for a small profit. Cigarettes were cheap but there was no market for them in the ville'. The locals always seemed to have plenty. I never got much past the instant coffee sales, so I didn't feel guilty. Many soldiers could not rein in their spending and began to get loans from Korean loan sharks in the village. This was a big mistake, if you did not pay up at the end of the month, you could expect to get shaken down at the front gate. If you had a long term unpaid debt you could get beaten up if you left the compound. Yobo would still let me crash at her hootch so my living expenses were minimal.

One day, a medic I barely knew, approached me with a strange offer. He asked me if I would like to participate in an all-nighter with his girlfriend. He promised me a female partner. "Where would this tryst take place?" I responded. At a cave he knew about in the local mountain. I immediately responded in the negative. Yobo had been pretty good to me and I had no desire to "butterfly" as the local girls called it. I thought this over for a day or two and realized Yobo was testing my loyalty. Most of the village girls would screw anyone with a thousand won, but if you had a steady, they were very jealous and would turn on you like a banshee if you strayed. There was always a great deal of tension among the men, fights were not infrequent. One day I witnessed a real fight. It was between SSgt Jones, the savior of the gay NCO, and a mess hall cook. The mess man was a good six inches taller than Jones and heavily muscled. Jones was getting in three punches to the cook's one. It was no contest. Jones finally landed a left hook to the jaw and the unfortunate dropped to the ground. He was conscious but unable to get up. This is the same Sergeant who picked up my discarded box of books and slipped them under his bed. One afternoon I was coming on duty and I heard the whine of a helicopter. The engine was literally screaming. The Piasecki H-21 "Shawnee" helicopter was a two bladed job known as the flying banana by the troops. It was supposedly retired in 1967 but they were still flying or rather attempting to fly in 1968. How they ever got off the ground still mystifies me. They were over age and outmoded but continued to ferry troops and equipment. I was afraid one would crash into the hospital. The helipad was only fifty yards from the entrance to the 642. The museum pieces the Air Force flew looked like prototypes of an abandoned design. One contraption had a bubble canopy and two counter rotating propellers on top. It looked like an over-sized mixmaster. My respect went out to the officer pilots who were forced to fly these death traps. (More on this later.)

We were required to turn out on a weekly basis for what was euphemistically referred to as 'training'. This was the sole responsibility of an SFC who did little else. There was no syllabus, no curriculum just 1950's vintage films on nuclear conflict and chemical biological war. No attempt was ever made to explain the Vietnam War. It was all about honoring our commitments. Since there was a new president in the Nam every few months, I failed to see how we could honor them. The NCO seemed to gain satisfaction in using the word training as a noun, pronoun, adjective or adverb. It went something like this, "I am Sgt. Caboose. Training will commence on a Training schedule set by the Training NCO to help you Train others to handle Training when the Trainer is unavailable". This may sound like an exaggeration, but it isn't. The Trainer was in love with the word. It was difficult to stifle a laugh when this character got started. Fortunately, when the lights went out and the black and white film began, you could catch some sleep. No tests were ever administered. There was really a lot of dead weight in the Army. At Ft. Sam Houston, Texas, an honest NCO told us why he remained in the Army. He had been drafted in WWII and became a medic. He served in Europe in a regimental aid station. After the War he reentered civilian life and got a factory job in his hometown. His work place was fairly noisy and he would get frequent headaches. One evening, in a local bar his migraine returned and he asked the bartender for several aspirin. Instead the man gave him two disinfectant tablets used to decontaminate the beer steins. He was violently ill for the next two days. The man re-upped a week later. I instantly understood, the Army was a haven, a place where he felt safe, a refuge from a harsh civilian environment. The Army was his womb. This gentleman was not the only career soldier who couldn't cut it in the civilian world. There were PTSD survivors who were given jobs as cadre. They gave instruction at the rifle ranges, or drove trucks. Some showed us how to pitch a platoon tent. No easy job. One of these sergeants wore the shoulder patch of the 36th Texas Division mauled in the Italian campaign. He was never quite focused, the eyes betrayed his distraction. He spoke to us but it seemed he was speaking to himself or no one. He was the face of a combat vet who had seen too much. Which brings me to the subject of the 642 psychiatrist. This gentleman was someone I never saw. Not once. He kept to himself and only communicated with the nurses and several enlisted medics. From what I could gather he was simply overwhelmed by the patients he had to deal with. He seldom interacted with the other Doctors and simply would go to his quarters and close the door. I do know that he was diagnosed with testicular cancer and died before he could be discharged from the medical corps. A tragic figure. Possibly he knew he was seriously ill.

All was not dismal, dull, or routine. There were occasional USO shows at the enlisted men's club. I only attended several because I was mostly a non-drinker. There were occasionally Philippine or Australian strippers that appeared to perform acts that were not the least bit erotic. Not that our libidos needed any encouragement. These ladies were bush league, no pun intended, and could not have made a living in their home countries. Bob Hope was another matter. I am writing this account a bit out of sequence, but since we are on the subject of entertainment it is appropriate to include his "performance" at Youngsan in December of 1968. Because of the limited space only ten men were allowed to go to the Christmas show. For once I was lucky. There was a drawing for tickets and I got one. We had to convey wheel chair patients to the show. It was a bit difficult to get the chairs into the blue busses but we arrived about one hour ahead of schedule. The troop had performed in Japan and on an aircraft carrier. Korea was the next stop. Mr. Hope arrived about one-half hour before the show and the Les Brown band about the same time. I do not wish to sully the reputation of the man, but he was very hard on his crew. His entire monologue was printed on huge cardboard cards. A grip would flip from card to card as the show progressed. The cards were huge three by four feet. He almost immediately began to yell at the technicians. "How the Hell am I going to read the goddamn cards if you've got a klieg light in my face? What idiot put all these cables on stage? You want me to break my neck?" I find it curious that no biography has emerged regarding this gentleman. I would not have volunteered to work for him. Mr. Hope made a fortune on these USO shows. Jet transportation was provided for free from the defense department. Many of the acts were volunteers like Miss World. Ann Margaret was the featured singer on this tour, and her husband Roger Smith never let her out of his sight. She appeared on stage in a mini-skirt and proved to be a good hoofer. Hope was an accomplished dancer and exhibited considerable grace for an old man. The soldiers and marines appeared to be positioning themselves to photograph Ms. Margaret from the feet up, rather than the bosom down. I knew exactly what these comedians were up to and had a good laugh. One GI, at a show later in the tour, got the photo he was after; it was never published. Mr. Hope was a very wealthy man. He supposedly owned more undeveloped land in California than any other celebrity. His estimated wealth was in the neighborhood of one billion dollars. In the comedy movies he made and produced, box lunches were provided. No caterer was ever contracted. He was reputed to be very thrifty. I was never a big fan of his brand of humor, but the troops seemed to enjoy the performance. Les Brown was a real gentleman and after the show left the stage to shake hands with the troops. When the cameras were not on, Bob appeared to be distant and unapproachable. I consider Mr. Hope to be a great American, he certainly was a morale builder of the first order.

Westmoreland was long gone by now, after the Tet Offensive he had asked for another 200,000 troops. President Johnson was not about to activate the 500,000 strong National Guard. This would have been politically impossible. Part of the price paid for the War is what I refer to as the "Vietnam derangement syndrome". The syndrome really began as a consequence of the Hollywood-ization of the War. We could have won it if we had only unleashed the full power of the military. The refrain: "Are you going to allow us to win this time?" began to appear on the silver screen. The soldier in the "Tiger Cage" was featured at Fourth of July parades. My God! Men are being held in captivity after we departed! This is an outrage! Numerous congressional committees journeyed to Vietnam to lay the myths to rest. Even John McCain was bold enough to suggest there were no more captives to be found. He was immediately branded a sell-out by those who chose to perpetuate the myth. Almost forty years after the cessation of hostilities, the taxpayers are still ponying up $30,000,000 a year in a fruitless search for any "remains." Remember, this princely sum is for the recovery of less than 2,500 missing. In the Pacific War, the dead sailors from ships that came under attack were simply sewn up in burlap bags and committed to the deep. I do not mean to denigrate the sacrifices of these gallant Americans, but to point out the impossibility of the task. The tropics decompose remains in a few weeks. My late father-in-law served in the 1st Marine Division at Peleliu in WWII. He said that after a week, the only way to distinguish between the dead Japanese and Americans was by their boots and leg wraps. The Marines wore laced leggings, the Japanese wore puttees. Before his death he denounced the search for the missing at a Division reunion. He stated it was fruitless and a waste of time and money. He was virtually ignored. Some of the veterans left the room.

The Moving Wall is another example of the inability or unwillingness of Vets to leave the War behind them. The Vietnam Memorial Wall is driven around the country and displayed at various parks during the year. The 58,000 names displayed are a miniature version of the Memorial in Washington. If such a monument memorialized the dead of WWII, it would have to be eight times larger. The American Veterans will never leave Jane Fonda alone. She will forever be: "Hanoi Jane, traitor bitch!" Looking for a scapegoat to blame for the loss will never end. It is not much different from Weimar Germany after the end of WWI. The "stab in the back" was delivered by mysterious political and social forces: the Communists, the Spartacists, the Jews. In the 1920's General Pershing, on a goodwill tour of South America, said to the officers of the Navy cruiser that took him to Argentina: "Germany suffered no real damage during the War, there were food shortages but nothing else. They never realized they were beaten. We should have marched down the Unter Den Linden in a victory parade. A few of our men would have been shot and killed but we would have apprehended the hold outs and hung them. We didn't beat them enough. We will have to do it all over again." And so we did. The Iraq war is a symptom of this "we are invincible" thought process. Since we have the most powerful and best trained military in the world, let the generals run the show. How can we lose?

An atypical example of the troops assigned to the 642 was Sp/5 Denton. He was the nephew of a powerful Senator from the South who was a close confidant of Lyndon Johnson. He made no secret of the fact that Senator Mumford had helped him to avoid Vietnam. The man lived large and seemed to have virtually limitless amounts of cash. His first coup was bedding the daughter of one of the Korean interpreters on base. She was a petite girl and most certainly disease free. Denton never ceased smiling, he would have been an ideal candidate for a toothpaste advertisement.

My friend, Tom Grimaldi, seemed to enjoy my antics with the senior enlisted men. He actually laughed so hard at times tears filled his eyes. He did not like them either, but had no desire to compromise his Spec/5 chevrons. Tom had entered the Army directly out of High School. He was unschooled but very intelligent. Me, a private, was "Boss," and this from a Sergeant! Tom was a good listener and a deadly poker player. No one could beat him. He was a card counter and something of a mathematical savant. After he cleaned out the senior enlisted men, the company officers decided to put him in his place. He wiped them out. For several years after getting out of the Army, he was a professional gambler in Las Vegas. Years later I asked him how he fared. He said, "After living expenses I broke even." Tom was something of a Jekyll and Hyde personality, but both faces were equally appealing. Off duty, he was constantly laughing and arguing with people. He was a stout defender of the War in Vietnam and criticized those of us who were against it. One day I got into a heated argument with him and he started swearing at me. I jumped over my bunk and grabbed his throat with both hands as if I was prepared to strangle him. We both dissolved in laughter and were close friends thereafter. Tom was the best friend I ever had. On duty, he was completely serious: a no nonsense pro who had the guts to yell at a physician if he observed a mistake. Once, an anesthesiologist at the hospital showed up impaired from a night of revelry. He was obviously hung over. Sergeant Grimaldi told Captain America to get out of the O.R. immediately or he would personally report him to the Hospital Commander. The Captain meekly obeyed. A few years after his Las Vegas experience, he began college and ultimately received a Bachelor's Degree in

Nursing and a Masters Degree in Public Health Administration. His entire family suffered from diabetes and he died of a heart attack at age sixty. He was and remains the most unforgettable character I ever met. I drove through a blizzard to attend his funeral in Ohio. Rest in Peace, dear friend!

I received the Chicago Daily News about two weeks late from my mother. This was one of the finest newspapers published in the United States. It was truly fair and balanced, and the editorial page was superb. Freedom of the press is one of the most precious gifts from the founding fathers. Reportage in the 1960's was superior to what we have now in America. The watch dogs of democracy have turned into the lap dogs of the oligarchy.

Tom Grimaldi came to me with a story that spelled real trouble for a young Filipino nurse. She was from a well to do family in Manila and had become pregnant by an infantry officer. The young lady was no beauty, and the officer had no intention of marrying her. In an advanced stage of pregnancy it was standard procedure to send these women home. She was deathly afraid of facing her family and especially her father. This was the 1960's and pregnancy out of wedlock was no laughing matter. Her fate was in the hands of the hospital commander and the 8th Army. It was common practice in those days to have exchange programs between countries viewed as allies of the United States. The nurse in question was part of this endeavor. She pleaded to be allowed to stay in Korea until the delivery date arrived. Here was yet another candidate for the Pearl S. Buck orphanage. I believe she was sent to the large American field hospital located on the Kanto plain in Japan. She was promptly placed on a departing aircraft and hustled off. A resident of Manila who knew the family stated it was best if she remained at Camp Zama.

By late autumn the Presidential Conventions were over, and the choice for next occupant of the white house was either Nixon or Humphrey. The Vice-President was burdened by the albatross of Vietnam and trod a very narrow path. He had to support Johnson's policies, yet leave a door open for withdrawal or negotiations. Nixon had a "secret plan" to end the War. The secret was trying to win it. Even as a sixteen year old I was a Kennedy supporter. Nixon always looked shifty and devious. Henry Kissinger had the best take on the future president: "I never understood how a man so uncomfortable around people could choose a career in public life." It came to light many years later that Dr. Kissinger was involved in a plot to derail the Paris Peace Talks in an effort to insure a Nixon victory. Johnson got wind of it and spoke of treason. America no longer speaks with one voice regarding foreign policy. Everyone is involved now.

The Vietnam War was going full tilt. The new field commander Creighton Abrams was asked by a reporter what he thought the future held, "I see more fighting," he replied, which was a sage observation. In Korea, a huge blood draw program was ongoing. You were given a little card embossed with a tube and an IV infusion set reaching from the Korean peninsula to Vietnam. At the time, over one thousand men per month were dying in combat. The Post basketball court was turned into a make shift blood center. I became a Master Phlebotomist: visible veins, rolling veins, invisible veins, no veins and yours truly could get blood out of them. Everyone was giving blood, every three months. Given the penchant of the troops to visit the local cat houses, Lord knows what invisible bugs were passed on to the poor wounded in Vietnam. I transfused one nurse and she returned the favor. The pint units of blood were spirited off to Kimpo for air transport to the Nam. It was a study in human weakness or bravery to watch these soldiers and Korean employees part with their precious bodily fluids. Some looked at the needle as if it were a medieval torture device. Their eyes widened and they barred their teeth. Others were quite nonchalant as if getting a routine injection. Only one or two passed out. Needles never bothered me, bullets, however, were another matter. The blood teams traveled throughout Korea looking for potential donors. The Air Force was hit hard. Being two hundred miles from the 38th parallel they were safe from any sudden shock or threat of hostile action. These men actually had curtains on the windows of their barracks! The Army was afforded no such amenities.

We were summoned in two separate groups to the tiny hospital theatre and given yet another pep talk on celibacy by a medical service officer. They must have drawn lots to see who would get the task. The Captain in question looked very uncomfortable. We were not shown any scary "You can go blind from casual sexual contact films." Rather, the approach to the topic was quite obtuse. The lecture was over in less than ten minutes and we went our separate ways. I spotted the good Captain several weeks later in the company of a young lady in Japanese village. This was where the high end talent resided. These girls were attractive and quite expensive. He certainly was showing restraint!

Chapter 11

Somehow it came down to us that a member of the Pueblo crew had been killed during the boarding of the ship. This may have been an embarrassment to the North Koreans. Months had passed and the negotiations continued. One day I was detailed with several other medics to deliver some supplies to a unit well off the beaten track. The roads were mostly unpaved and we bounced along for some miles before we reached our destination. This base was really primitive. The troops were living in tents with wooden sides. The latrine was a large trench dug into the hard earth. It was now late autumn and getting cold. Relieving yourself was a challenge. Needless to say it was also accomplished quickly. I asked the guard at the gate what the site was supposed to achieve, he waved me off. It was a Pershing One missile battery. They were guarding a nuclear missile site! I had never seen a nuclear weapon before or since. The Pershings were deployed under large canvas tarps on the trailers of very large trucks. I asked, "So this is a nuclear weapon site?"

The guard answered, "You didn't see me and I didn't talk to you."

Obviously this kid was under orders to remain silent. We returned to the 642. It was dark by the time we pulled into the motor pool. At the time of the seizure of the Pueblo, there were no American fighter aircraft in Korea armed with guns. The F-100's had bomb shackles that would only accommodate nuclear weapons. The missiles they carried were air to air sidewinders that were made for shooting down enemy aircraft. The only thing we could have accomplished would have been to provide Air Cover while the captured ship steamed toward Wonsan Harbor. This was one mistake the Navy was reluctant to discuss after the seizure. Boarding an American ship by an enemy was something that had

not happened since the War of 1812. The Navy brass was

understandably upset. All of this, of course, was unknown at the time.

In World War II they referred to losing touch with home and family as "going Asiatic." I was getting there. Home and hearth were becoming abstractions. I was learning Korean a little at a time. The locals' conversations were no longer indecipherable. When I returned home, I went to a Korean restaurant for a meal. The diners were bilingual. They spoke Korean to each other and I surmised they were trying to stick me with their bill. I left immediately. Mrs. Kim and I got along well when I worked nights, and she pretty much ceded control of the wards to me. I was able to keep the lid on most of the time, and experienced no more ward riots.

There were more marriage requests from enlisted men. The military discouraged interracial marriages between soldiers and locals. Most decent women would have nothing to do with Americans, so it was assumed that the future wives were prostitutes. Most were, but they still made acceptable wives. Go to any Army base in the United States and you will find Korean restaurants, convenience stores, liquor stores and the like. The GIs not only came over with their newly minted wives, but the entire family. It was "hands across the sea," so to speak. Captain Sideburns flipped out one day. A GI wanted to marry his Korean sweetheart shortly after getting a serious case of clap from her. Greater love hath no man. Whether this unholy alliance was ever consummated I do not know. Suffice to say, love will find a way. At this point in my Army career, nothing surprised me.

The rumors were rife. There was a new "hostess" at the showboat club and she had blue eyes and brown hair! This latest attraction had to be seen to be believed. The Oklahoma Land Rush of 1889 had nothing on the mad dash to get to the village. Everyone off-duty and apparently at least two on-duty made it to the club the next evening. I arrived late and was unable to gain entrance for at least one hour. I finally squeezed in and sure enough, she did have blue eyes. Apparently, some American serving in Korea after WWII had impregnated a woman and the result was a Caucasian. No evidence of Oriental DNA was visible. The young lady in question was no beauty, but the novelty of it was beyond unique. Apparently, she was unable to speak any English, which further deepened the mystery. Had Miss Universe showed up, she could hardly have attracted more attention. Her presence in the club continued for several more days, then she disappeared as mysteriously as she had arrived. The gossip was that her services were purchased by a high ranking officer who had sufficient cash to afford her companionship. I realize my description of this human trafficking might sound disgusting to you, but remember, we were all in our twenties with raging hormones. Judeo-Christian morals and mores were meaningless in the Orient. Sex was just another commodity to be bought and sold. From a distance of over forty years it still seems incredible.

There was a distillation unit located in the operating room. It supplied mineral free water for surgery. The water was autoclaved and subsequently used for irrigation during operations. It became apparent to the head nurse that the boiling water still could not keep up with the demand. Someone was filching the water for drinking purposes. A word about the available water supply; it was awful. Heavily chlorinated and faintly yellow in color, the troops believed it was piped in directly from the latrine. Others believed it came from the rice paddies. In any event, the water theft had to be brought to a halt. We were a surgical hospital and the welfare of our patients was priority number one. In this regard everyone was in total agreement. The thefts had to stop. An announcement was made and posted on the bulletin board, "The unauthorized consumption of distilled water will not be tolerated, anyone found in the operating room without authorization will be Court Martialed!" This may sound a bit harsh, but it could not continue. Whether or not the thief was apprehended I do not know. The rumor was the officers were helping themselves to the supply for mixed drinks. A guard was finally posted after hours to keep an eye on the still which operated 24/7. The head surgical nurse was a no-nonsense Georgian with a heavy drawl. The Major was regular Army and kept the nurses and physicians in line. She had spent a year in Vietnam and was disgusted by what she had witnessed. Somehow Major Clark got the idea that Westmoreland should have been replaced by Moshe Dayan. Dayan was her hero. The Six Day War in 1967 was the exemplar of how wars should be fought. She mentioned his name frequently with something approaching awe. There were no war lovers in the Army Medical Corps, most had seen its face close up and were all for the Paris Peace Talks. There was actual applause in the hospital when the Americans sat down with the North Vietnamese as it was announced over radio Tomahawk.

You may get the idea that the enlisted members attached to the hospital were a bunch of hyperactive sex fiends. Nothing could be further from the truth. Some of the enlisted men had college degrees and a few O.R. techs were working on their PhDs when Uncle Sam called. A close friend of mine was Ralph Watson, who was working on his Doctorate when drafted. His wife was a stunning model who posed for clothing ads in his native Indiana. It was very enjoyable to converse with this low key gentleman. He never frequented the village and seldom drank. During off hours, he spent most of his time reading. We had two pharmacists one of whom refused to accept a commission. He was a Sergeant. The reason for his enlisted status was simple. Reserve officers had to serve three consecutive years in the Army. By refusing a commission the young man only had to serve two years. He was most anxious to return to his wife and infant child. Another O.R. tech was a very handsome Reform Jew. He was also a two year draftee sent to MFSS due to his high intelligence. He was married but took up with a beautiful high class hooker in JV. This affair went on for some time until he broke it off. He was a wise young man and his girlfriend would take no money. I envied his looks, several other hostesses offered their services gratis but he demurred.

The winds coming down from Manchuria signaled the approach of my second winter in Korea. Snow was not only welcomed but wished for by the infantrymen along the DMZ. If there were any North Korean infiltrators crossing the 38th Parallel it was a simple matter to track them. November and December were the best months, virtually no hostile ambushes or casualties. At about this time it was decided that we medics had to qualify with the M-14 rifle. I had not fired a weapon in over a year, and to choose cold weather to snap in with a rifle bespoke poor planning. One Saturday, about half the company was issued rifles and told to clean them. It was unnecessary to clean them as they were spotless. The real task was to remove the oil which we had slathered them with on a weekly basis. My weapon was like a greased pig. It took some effort to wipe off the linseed oil on the stock. We climbed into the backs of two and one half ton trucks bearing our weapons and drove out to the site. I did not know how far it was to the rifle range and neglected to put on my long underwear. It took us over an hour to reach our destination. By the time we arrived my teeth were chattering, and my knees were knocking together like castanets. I did not believe I could hit a barn door because of my approaching hypothermia. The trucks had canvas sides and the cold winds blew on us for the entire journey. When we disembarked we walked to the firing line and were issued one twenty round magazine with seven rounds! Like so much else in the Army this was an exercise in futility, it takes at least five rounds minimum to zero a high powered rifle. The targets were Bull's Eyes fixed at fifty yards. This is a piddling distance for a military rifle. Fortunately, some thoughtful soul had started wood fires in 55 gallon drums so we could warm up. We were to fire all seven rounds from the prone position. Ten of us assumed the position and began squeezing the triggers. My eyes had started to tear up because of the cold, and hugging the butt of the weapon my glasses steamed up. The ground was icy. I carefully squeezed off the seven shots. A cease fire was called and the targets were inspected. I had achieved the approximate center of the target, but about a foot above the bulls eye. The elevation was set too high. The supervising NCO checked the rifles to make sure they were empty, and we hustled over to the flaming oil drums to warm up. The entire process lasted for at least one and a half hours.

We finally boarded the trucks and returned to the 642. When we got off the deuce and a half, we went to the arms room and cleaned our rifles. I quickly hustled off to the hospital and took a long hot shower. We pitied the men on the DMZ at this time of year. They were afforded no such luxuries

Speaking of the DMZ, in cold weather it was difficult to stay awake at night. Sleeping on guard is considered to be a court martial offense. It has to be. If an infiltrator happened on a sleeping soldier he would never wake up. They carried knives and did not hesitate to use them. From my description of the senior enlisted men you may have gathered they were not well respected. Most were in their forties and were well past the age for duty with the infantry.

There has been a lot of propaganda over the years that the U.S. Army of the 60s was made up of volunteers. This was not the case. Most of the infantrymen in Vietnam were draftees. The lack of NCOs who could cut it in the field was limitless so the Army created the so called shake-and-bake NCO schools overseas. For a period of six or eight weeks the prospective sergeants attended non-commissioned-officer school. Upon graduation these men were issued the chevrons of a sergeant and given command of a squad. Remarkably, the system worked quite well. I attended one 2nd Division reunion in 1998 and spoke to several of these people. They performed adequately, by and large, and got the cooperation of their subordinates. One Sergeant told me a story that is illustrative of the difficulty of staying awake at night. On this occasion he approached the fox hole of a sleeping soldier and shook him awake. This position was scant yards away from the fence that marked the beginning of the DMZ. The soldier was half in and half out of his sleeping bag with his loaded rifle laying on the ground outside the hole. The sergeant warned him that such a breach of security a second time would warrant disciplinary action. He walked away and shortly thereafter a shot rang out. The disgruntled GI had fired a round in the general direction of his Superior. He turned on his heel and ran back to the foxhole and dragged the man out by his collar. The offending GI was taken to the nearest bunker and the 1st Sergeant awakened. "This man took a shot at me and I want to get rid of him now!" Confronting an angry man with a loaded weapon takes guts. This sergeant was a real leader. What happened to the sleeping GI afterward? I do not know. Out of sight! Out of mind! He was gone in the morning.

It was not lost on the men overseas that a substantial reservoir of National Guard troops and enlisted reserve were never called to active duty. The George Bushes of the world were all for defeating the Communist Menace in the Far East as long as others were called upon to shoulder the burdens and dangers of active duty. Dick 'five deferments" Cheney had "other priorities", as he put it. I did not dwell on this inequity much in my twenties. Compulsory military service for all would give future politicians pause before getting the nation involved in war.

The zero defects go-go Army of the 1960s was understandable in terms of our trip to the rifle range. The boxes were checked off, everything was properly accounted for and nothing was gained. There was a group think process going on that guaranteed a lack of critical thinking. Winter was approaching and jerry cans of kerosene began appearing around the compound. The Koreans had a unique method of heating their homes. Very small coal heaters began appearing in the hootches. They were about the size of a fifteen gallon garbage can. Cylindrical coal blocks which had numerous holes drilled all the way through them, were inserted into the cans. When one began to turn white, a second was put on top and the heat from the depleted first cylinder set the second alight. In many homes the exhaust flues ran under the house. If there was any leakage of exhaust gas everyone inside could be killed from carbon monoxide. In this way the floors could be kept toasty warm but the risks involved were considerable. The Korean government was well aware of the problem and offered a large financial reward to anyone who could invent a carbon monoxide sensor. The resulting device is now widely available in the United States and undoubtedly popular in the Far East.

With the arrival of cold weather, we suddenly began to receive ammunition: a lot of ammunition. Steel and wood boxes with steel straps were off loaded from deuce and a half trucks and placed in above ground bunkers and an armored personnel carrier appeared mounting a .50 caliber machine gun. What was going on? Down from Camp Casey came the answer. A soldier showed up with a complete shoulder separation. He was wearing a sling and it was evident that he was in pain. It turns out his unit had come under attack. The North Koreans had fired several mortar rounds and machine gunned a few barracks. He wanted to access the locked arms room and was unable to find the clerk who had the key. Undaunted, he secured a fire ax and began to attack the door. Entry into the Quonset hut was not difficult but the weapons were behind a padlocked steel door. He began to flail away at the lock and this is where he separated his shoulder. He was able to force an entry and the arms and ammunition were distributed. The North Koreans fled soon after. This was the nature of the attacks launched on Korean and American forces in 1966-69. Hit and run. Fire a burst or two from a sub-machine gun and disappear into the night. The GI who forced entry into the arms room should have gotten a medal. Possibly he did.

The night patrols in those days were risky propositions. A soldier had a much better chance of getting shot by a jittery companion than the NKPA. Accidental discharges were not uncommon. Theoretically, a loaded weapon should be kept on safe until the moment of firing. This was not always the case. The M-14 rifle had the safety inside the trigger guard. It was a simple matter to disengage it; just snap it forward. Often the soldier simply forgot to utilize it. If he tripped or the weapon was snagged in some shrubbery, "bang"! It was an accidental discharge. One poor nineteen year old draftee propped his rifle against the fender of a truck and it fell over. It discharged and entered and exited his left thigh. Somehow it shattered his femur but failed to sever the femoral artery. Some months later I observed him talking to the physician who had performed the operation. He said, "I am sorry,

Son. You are going to walk with a slight limp for the rest of your life. Your left leg is now at least one and a half inches shorter than your right." The Army is always reluctant to release figures on friendly fire incidents, but we were doing a far better job of killing and wounding each other than the North Koreans.

The first snows came in early November. One day, I was on my way to the Post Library to return a book. The library was on the top of a small knoll. I was about fifty feet from the door when a jet screamed overhead at about two hundred feet. I dove, head first into a small mound of snow and covered my head. The F-4 Phantom was a big loud aircraft and did a slow roll over the hospital. I was mad as hell because my uniform was now wet and grimy from the mixture of snow and dirt. Buzzing a military compound was a serious breach of Air Force policy. Who would be brazen enough to try such a stunt and get away with it? I found out years later that Chuck Yeager was stationed at Kunsan AFB south of us. He was the only Air Force officer who could successfully get away with such a stunt.

The temperature had dropped sufficiently so it was no longer necessary to walk in the mud of Bupyong. The paddy fields were rock hard now, and the only visible remnants of the rice crop were the stubs of harvested plants. We went on alert yet again in anticipation of the return of the Pueblo crew, another false alarm. The houseboys that worked in our huts were no longer washing our clothes. A laundry had been installed. Formerly, our greens were dumped in a 55 gallon drum filled with water and detergent. The houseboys would strip to their underwear and jump in agitating the mix as a winery worker might crush grapes; not very efficient. The laundry was a welcome addition as our clothing really took a beating from the old method. By now my fatigues were very faded; the sign of a true veteran. We would have appreciated the issue of Parkas but none were given to troops in the rear. As stated earlier, new shoes or uniforms were difficult to obtain. The initial issue in basic training was still adorning our backs and feet. I found a pair of abandoned boots in a garbage can one day. They were size thirteen, I wore a twelve but they were a

Godsend. I put toilet paper in the toes and wore them. With woolen socks they were reasonably comfortable. I wore my new footgear on duty although you were really supposed to don oxfords. I wanted to save my expensive low quarters for inspections.

General Bonesteel's strategy for dealing with the North Korean infiltration and sabotage seemed to be working. Now that the winter snows arrived the 8th Army could relax a bit. The NKPA may have been crazy, but they weren't stupid. Leaving tracks in the snow did not guarantee a long life. Over two hundred North Korean saboteurs were killed in 1968 alone. If it had not been for the cooperation of the South Korean people, the outcome may have been quite different.

The acrid aroma emanating from the chimneys around the village indicated almost total reliance on coal for fuel. In the hinterlands, the hills were denuded of any vegetation that could be used for cooking or heating.

We were finally getting some helicopters; the Huey was the staple helicopter of the Vietnam War. In February 1968, there was only one available to the 8th Army. The rest were museum pieces, overage and underpowered. By early 1969 eight were available. The flight crews were well trained and kept the birds in A-1 condition. How many lives were saved by the prompt evacuation of the wounded will probably never be known. Suffice to say the crews of these aircraft were very brave and dedicated.

One day I was dispatched to the maternity hospital in Bupyong with some supplies that were urgently needed. I accompanied a nurse and a physician. What the 642 donated to the locals I no longer recall. What I do remember were the crude conditions available for pregnant women. The delivery room had cement floors that were angled in such a way as to allow drainage into a large cavity in the center. The walls were set in white tiles and there was a single lighting fixture in the ceiling. Primitive would be too generous a word to use. The delivery couch had the usual stirrups but the room seemed to lack any other amenities. I knew the Koreans were tough but this hospital was really something to behold. Americans can never really experience a Third World country unless they see it first-hand. The strides the nation has made in the last forty-six years are truly remarkable. Seoul is a modern city with a thriving economy. One need only to compare it to North Korea; a closed Stalinist society that cannot feed its own people.

Thanks to the very insightful articles in the National Geographic Magazine I began to fully appreciate the complete failure of communism in the North. Cannibalism was even practiced in many communities. The country was filled with informers, even the smallest criticism of the government could land a person in a work camp gulag. Starvation in the mid-nineties may have resulted in the deaths of several million people. The Hermit Kingdom got its name in the nineteenth century. The Kim Il Sung dynasty was answerable to no one. China exercises minimal pressure on the regime, they are completely isolated from the rest of the world. How long this can continue is anyone's guess. It is a land truly frozen in time.

Chapter 12

April 1968

The Chief's autopsy was conducted by Dr. Stanfield. I was allowed to read it. "Multiple fractures of the cranium, fragments of bone penetrating the frontal cerebrum. Fracture of the left femur." Apparently the Chief's head had struck one of the pilings before it entered the creek. There was no water in the lungs. He had stopped breathing as a result of the head injury. After reading the report Dr. Stanfield put his arm around me and said, "Nothing could have been accomplished by CPR, the head injury was lethal." I never forgot this kind gesture. He was, in essence, absolving me of any guilt. The Chief had left the hospital without signing the company pass book. He was essentially AWOL. The entire complement of men that signed out that night had to do it again. The company pass roster was torn out and the Chief's name was forged by the Company Commander. Everyone signed the blank page in the sequence they had earlier departed the hospital. The family of the dead soldier would receive $10,000 in life insurance of the now officially off-duty medic. Captain Jonas risked his career on the deception. He wanted the family to get the money. The man had a heart. I hope he had a good life.

****

December 1968

Rumors began to circulate that the Pueblo crew would soon be released. Apparently the Captain and crew were now sufficiently contrite to receive mercy from the "Dear Leader". December 23, 1968 dawned crisp and cold. The Pueblo crew was returning. Our helipad was cleared of snow and we prepared for the imminent arrival of the crew. A correspondent from NBC News named Grant Wolfkill was present at the hospital and I spoke to him briefly. The head nurse had lectured us and essentially said we were not to talk to any of the reporters under any circumstances. We learned that one of the crew members had died. His name was Duane Hodges. He had been killed by a cannon shell that passed through the hull of the ship when Commander Bucher had refused to heave to during the seizure. Admiral Edwin M. Rosenberg had arrived at the 642 to greet the inbound crew. I had never seen an admiral before. A gaggle of Navy officers were also in attendance including physicians.

The helicopters began arriving early in the afternoon, a Navy band greeted the arriving sailors with a spirited rendering of "Anchors Away". I had never seen so many Hueys before. Snow had been carefully removed to prevent it from blowing in the faces of the numerous media people in attendance. The crew was hustled into the hospital and immediately were issued blue nuclear submarine coveralls with "Pueblo" emblazoned on the back. About twelve of the crew were assigned to my ward. I was not on duty, but was dressed in hospital whites. The medical checks began almost immediately. The entire crew appeared to be wan and very pale. I went on duty several hours before my normal shift. The crew was asking for spiked eggnog. This was clearly not a viable option before the physicians gave them a through medical check. One sailor approached me and asked if I would look at his foot. The men were all wearing cloth hospital sandals. He took his off and let me examine his feet. His right foot was blue green in color with the hematoma extending from his great toe to his instep. I was reasonably sure several bones in it were broken. I said, "You should have an x-ray of that foot done immediately." He waved me off and said, "I want to get back to the states as soon as possible, please don't say anything. They promised to get us back home by Christmas Eve." I realized that for us it was December 23rd. If they departed by jet flying east, a day would be gained by crossing the International Dateline. I kept quiet. One of the sailors asked me if it was possible to get him an ice cream cone. I said that the mess hall was open and I would see what could be done. I got the cone and brought it back to the ward. Passing a nurse in the hall who was wiping tears from her eyes, my imagination centered on what condition the other crew members were in. It turned out the complete military records of the crew were captured with the ship. The men were all subjected to beatings but one petty officer was singled out for special treatment. The man had attended a C.I.C. school which stood for Combat Information Center. The North Koreans immediately interpreted this as C.I.A. The punishment meted out to him was especially severe. There was a waiting line for hot showers. I entered the bathroom with towels and noticed that the backs of the men bore evidence of recent beatings. The black and blue marks bore mute testimony to the treatment they received shortly before release.

After the medical checks, the men settled down and wanted to know what was happening in the States. My knowledge of recent events was limited because I had been away from home about as long as they had been prisoners. Ten months in-country was a long gap to be bridged. Admiral Rosenberg entered the ward and extended his hand. "I appreciate everything you are doing to make the men comfortable," stated the Admiral. Navy protocol differed significantly from the Army. Generals generally do not shake hands with privates. A call came over the P.A. system asking if any duty medics came from Seattle, San Francisco, Denver, and Chicago. Since my hometown was close enough to Chicago to qualify I approached the head nurse and said that I was from Illinois. I spoke to a young sailor from Niles, Illinois and told him that I didn't have much to say regarding hometown news. My ignorance was only compounded by saying Mayor Daley was still in charge.

The hours passed and it grew dark. Most of the men were so excited to be free that they found it difficult to settle in for the night. One young man asked me to sit down and talk. By this time it was lights out. Urging the sailor to get to sleep, he said, "I am too happy to sleep!" He proceeded to regale me with stories about his imprisonment. Apparently one of the North Korean female guards fell in love with a curly, blond-haired sailor. She made it a point to give him extra food and always smiled at him when no one was around. The funniest story was related to me about a North Korean soldier who was stealing fruit from the prisoners. One of the sailors put numerous pin holes in an apple and soaked it overnight in a bowl of his own urine. He smoothed the apple with his thumb to disguise the pin holes, and placed it on a table next to his bunk. The following day the crew was taken out of their cells for routine exercise. Returning to his quarters the apple had disappeared. The thief did not return to guard duty for days.

The obscene gesture reported by Time magazine cost them dearly. "Hell Week" was the most memorable and painful experience in their eleven month confinement. Kicking is a universal practice in both Koreas. The NKPA were experts in delivering blows where the pain would be excruciating. The shins and backs were the primary targets for punishment. The abuse continued for days until one member of the crew decided to end it. There was a small contingent of Korean language interpreters on the ship, one of them slashed his wrists in protest over the beatings. He apparently used the lid from a can of food. The North Koreans panicked; the punishment ceased. At the 642 Hospital, the man who attempted suicide was strictly segregated from the hospital staff and fellow crew members. Naval intelligence gave him a thorough de-briefing so I will refrain from revealing his identity.

It is very difficult to explain the anger we felt toward the Communists. If an order had been given to march across the 38th Parallel and begin shooting at them, everyone would have volunteered. The program of "enhanced interrogation" practiced by the Bush/Cheney regime would have been roundly denounced by anyone who served in the 642. Torture is a two-edged sword. The victim will tell you anything you want to hear and, all the while, plan revenge. Anyone who says torture saves lives and prevents future attacks is lying. Torture in Vietnam was not uncommon; the population was alienated and hearts and minds were never "won".

The young man who would not go to sleep regaled me with stories of how he was going to have special toilet paper made with Kim Il Sung's picture on each sheet. What struck me most about the Pueblo crew was their intelligence. Many had gone to college and they were well above-average for enlisted men. The sailors spoke among themselves about their captors. The guards and officers all had nick-names. "Super-C", "Deputy Dawg" and "Glorious General" were some of the names I heard. Five full wards in the hospital were devoted to the crew. They were in remarkably good condition considering the treatment they had received. Each of the crew members was later awarded a much deserved Purple Heart. I sensed a certain tension among the crew. They all were somewhat concerned about what awaited them back in the States. Men with wives and girlfriends wondered aloud about how they would be received. We had no idea what awaited Commander Bucher upon his return.

The Court of Inquiry that resulted from the capture of U.S.S. Pueblo was a shock to all of us. To even consider a Court Martial of the gallant commander seemed a travesty. The Navy holds sacred that a United States ship should never be boarded by an armed enemy. The fact that the ship was fired on with cannon and a sailor was killed seemed to mean very little. The question was asked over and over again, "Why did you allow the North Koreans to board your ship without a fight?" Fight with what? The North Koreans had cannon equipped torpedo boats quite capable of sinking the Pueblo. In addition, North Korean jet aircraft overflew the ship during the capture. Resistance would have resulted in many casualties plus the real possibility of sinking the ship in shallow coastal waters. The Sea of Japan in January is about 33 degrees Fahrenheit. The bottom line was the Pueblo was not a "Man of War". It was a ship tasked to gather electronic communications from the North. The crew was instructed to wear civilian attire when above decks and considering the War in Vietnam was ongoing at the time, the North Koreans considered it a provocation. Thumbing your nose at a nation of xenophobes could not be tolerated. The North Koreans meant business!

The next day the crew boarded helicopters for Kimpo where they boarded Air Force transports for the journey back to the States. The problems for Commander Bucher were just beginning. A Court of Inquiry was convened to conduct an investigation into the circumstances surrounding the seizure. The Navy seemed to be fixated on the fact that a U.S Navy ship was boarded and seized by an enemy power. The Pueblo carried Thompson sub-machine guns and a .50 Caliber machine gun unshielded on the deck. The Navy department wanted to know why the Captain failed to use them. The fact that the heavily armed North Koreans would have sunk the ship if fired on failed to move them. Further, the Pueblo was a cargo vessel of the same type that appears in the movie "Mr. Roberts"; hardly a "Man-o-War". Finally the Court of Inquiry recommended a trial by General Court Martial for the alleged offenses. As follows: 1.) Permitting his ship to be searched while he had the power to resist; 2.) Failing to take immediate and aggressive protective measures when his ship was attacked by North Korean Forces; 3.) Complying with the orders of the North Korean forces to follow them into port; 4.) Negligently failing to completely destroy all classified material aboard the USS Pueblo and permitting such material to go into the hands of the North Koreans; 5.) Negligently failing to insure, before departure for sea, that his officers and crew were properly organized, stationed and trained for emergency destruction of classified material. Apparently the death of one of the crew members failed to impress the Admirals who sat on the Court. The staff of the 642 could not believe it. I could not conceive of a situation where the Captain and crew could have acted differently. Fortunately, cooler heads prevailed. The Court Martial was later changed to a Letter of Reprimand which was cancelled by the Secretary of the Navy John H. Chaffee. He stated, "They have suffered enough." Sending a virtually unarmed ship into the territorial waters of a hostile nation bent of the destruction of the

South Korean government was a fool's errand. Incredibly, the Pueblo was unaware that a commando team from the North got to within two hundred yards of the President's house before being cut down by South Korean police. This incident, known as the Blue House Raid, resulted in the deaths of sixty-six people. Three days after the terrorist assassination attempt on President Park, the Pueblo was seized. Incredibly, the Navy failed to alert the ship that an Act of War had occurred days earlier. The gallant crew of the Pueblo suffered for eleven months due to this intelligence failure. Commander Bucher later stated, "Had I known about the Blue House Raid, I would have maneuvered my ship well away from the coast."

One could make the case that the attacks of 9/11 could have been prevented had the C.I.A. been working in concert with the F.B.I. A flight training school in Florida contacted the F.B.I and stated, "We have a group of Arabs down here who want to learn how to fly a commercial jet. They have no interest in take-offs and landings." The C.I.A. had Mohammed Atta on its terrorist watch list. Incredibly, there was no liaison between these two agencies.

The release of the Pueblo crew resulted in a palpable reduction of tensions along the DMZ. There would be no general war. The hospital staff was as one in condemnation of the manner in which the Pueblo incident was handled. Scapegoating seems to be a universal practice in military organizations. Someone must take the blame and Commander Bucher was no exception. Admiral Rosenberg recommended him for the Medal of Honor, needless to say, given the mindset of the Navy, this was out of the question. Looking back on these happenings after the passage of over forty years it seems incredible to me that we could have launched a large and costly war in Iraq on such faulty intelligence. During the Cuban missile crisis of 1962, Adlai Stevenson had photos of the weapons in Cuba. Colin Powell had cartoon renderings of the alleged "mobile chemical labs" to present to the U.N. We have, to date, spent something on the order of two trillion dollars on the Iraq and Afghanistan wars with little to show for our efforts.

Chapter 13

Another winter in Korea. The barracks' kerosene space heaters had a penchant for going out in the middle of the night. I slept under two woolen blankets, some men slept in their down sleeping bags. Frequently I would awaken in the morning and the barracks would be ice-cold. It surprised me how rapidly one could get dressed in such an environment. If nature called in the middle of the night, the latrine was fifty yards away from my barrack. Even in the dead of winter, I seldom put on my boots. Flip flops were the order of the day, even in deep snow. When you are young, you can get used to anything. Rather than the occasional gun shot or shrapnel wounds, we now received cases of frost bite. The parkas provided for infantrymen were reasonably warm, and if a man kept moving the chances of frostbite were not great. Carelessness was often the culprit. My mother purchased an olive drab parka and shipped it to me. It was close enough to Army issue that I wore it instead of my field jacket on very cold days. I visited Yobo a few times and met her brother who lived near Seoul. He seemed friendly enough although it was an awkward meeting. There was now almost a complete turn-over of staff at the 642. I made no effort to get acquainted with the new physicians and medics. Too much had occurred that year and the new people were largely unaware of what had happened in 1968. Since winter had settled in once again, we were given orders to remove all the residual oil from our rifles. The prevailing opinion being that the lubricant would freeze in the bitter conditions. By now taking apart the M-14 rifle was a task I could accomplish in a few minutes. Finishing the job, I raised the weapon to my shoulder and sighted the empty rifle at a telephone pole outside the arms room. The new clerk was a Vietnam returnee who objected to my raising the weapon and told me to rack it and leave. The next day I got a call from the new Company Commander who replaced Sideburns. "Why did you point your rifle out the window, Private?" I couldn't believe it! The asshole had actually reported me for raising the weapon and pointing it out a window! I did not even squeeze the trigger! Was this jerk trying to gain some brownie points with an officer at my expense? I shuffled a little and said I would never do it again. Had Captain Sideburns been sitting behind the desk I probably would have been given another Article 15 and fined. In the Army, the chicken shit never ended. The life of an enlisted man was filled with constant minor indignities that, in the aggregate, kept you on edge. The clerk became a standing joke. He was marked off as another "doofuss" who was not, by any means, bending the needle on the I.Q. meter. About this time the re-up NCO was making the rounds inquiring as to the possibility of signing up for another three years with the promise of a re-enlistment bonus! They actually approached me with an offer to go Regular Army! I would have preferred to go over Niagara Falls without a barrel rather than re-up and go to Vietnam. The Army in 1969 was hemorrhaging officers and enlisted men at such a rapid rate, anyone was eligible for another chance. Four men from the company actually opted for another three year hitch. They were very young and had no prospects in civilian life.

On duty, one afternoon, a Spec/4 showed up on our ward with no visible ailments, he was about thirty-five years old. He had large eyes and very long eye-lashes and appeared like the proverbial doe caught in the headlights. The upshot of this new admission was that he suffered from depression. The cause of his malady was a lack of promotion. He had a stateside wife and two children and was stuck with the rank of an E-4. No way was this gentle soul ever going to become an NCO. The Army had rejected him as Sergeant material but he refused to get the message. The Army was his career, and he was not prepared to face the uncertainties of civilian life. This unfortunate became a standing joke, a thirty-five year old Spec/4! I found nothing amusing about his predicament and tried to deflect the contempt others showed him. He spent about a week in the hospital and was discharged. Four days later he was back on the ward in worse mental shape than before. Apparently he had become the butt of derision in his unit, and the harassment had become unbearable. After one more week of bed rest he was released. What eventually happened to this poor lost soul - I will never know. I hope he was given a discharge. Life in the Army had become intolerable for him. There were other forms of career ending scenarios playing out. A Black Sergeant showed up with a blood pressure reading of 200/110. Stroke city! The Sergeant had received a letter from his wife stating his sixteen year old daughter was pregnant. This announcement, coupled with his difficulties keeping reluctant infantrymen in line, put him over the edge. Bed rest and medication brought his blood pressure down but a return to his Unit would cause it to spike again. Everyone was concerned he would stroke out before discharge. He should have been sent back to the States. He wasn't.

There is a saying inscribed in stone by some anonymous British soldier in the Rock of Gibraltar, "God and the soldier, all men adore in time of trouble and no more, for when war is over and all things righted, God is neglected, the old soldier slighted." There was no adoration of the soldier in the 60s the Vietnam War was playing out to an increasingly restive civilian population. None of us knew at the time that the new occupant of the White House had a plan to end the War. It was called Vietnam-ization. The War which had become an almost exclusive American enterprise was now going to be turned over to our allies. The fact that 500,000 Americans couldn't do the job, and a solo effort by our now traumatized allies was dubious, Nixon forged ahead. A draftee in the American Army faced a six year military commitment: two years active duty plus four in the standby reserve. It was obvious that the Chinese could enter the fray which would certainly result in a longer stint overseas. This was always in the back of my mind. No one ever talked about it. Strategy should never be a concern of a humble enlisted man. I had already made the decision that once I got back to the States they would never get me overseas again. I had enough.

The all volunteer Army is a terrible mistake. Repeated deployments of soldiers and marines are setting up a scenario for lifelong PTSD. The average period for an infantryman in World War II was two-hundred days, after which they were either dead, wounded, or crazy. Men who lost limbs in combat were actually happy to get out of danger. Their war was essentially over.

By this point in time, the extra duty roster was being filled by others. Most senior enlisted men had given up. They were incapable of turning me into a model soldier. It became obvious that they were avoiding me completely. Captain Sideburns did not complete his thirteen month tour. The rumor was that he had requested transfer to Vietnam. The new Company Commander was not overly concerned with haircuts, his specialty was shoes and brass buckles. One's branch of service was indicated by roundels on the collar: Crossed rifles for infantry, crossed cannons for artillery, the caduceus for medical corps. The so called round brass on the collars was prone to tarnish, so they had to be polished. This was not an easy task as the branch portion had to be detached from the flat part and tended to separately. I had not worn my Class A uniform since my arrival in Korea almost a year earlier. Out came the can of brasso and we diligently began to shine our belt buckles, and collar brass. After the uniforms were pressed, nothing happened. We never turned out for another formal inspection. Possibly the arrival of the reviewing team was cancelled. No one seemed upset. What we did do infrequently was "police call" which involved cleaning up the area outside the hospital by hand, no brooms. Cigarette butts were the primary source of detritus around the base. In theory you were supposed to field strip the used cigarettes and separate the paper from the tobacco. This supposedly got rid of the evidence, but the advent of the filter tip changed all that. The pesky filters littered the area, and had to be cleaned up by hand. This is very demeaning work, especially in cold weather. The officers did not participate in these activities; only the lowly enlisted people. The theory was that police calls reminded us of who we were: enlisted coolies. The indignities suffered by troops were too many to elaborate, but probably pre-dated the Punic Wars. The only thing missing was the cat-of-nine-tails. Tom Grimaldi was one of the few enlisted men remaining in country that I still knew well. Occasionally, I saw Yobo. There were no more irrational scenes with which to cope. She only asked me for money once and I pointed out that additional compensation was not possible. There were no hard feelings.

The Christmas edition of The Pacific Stars and Stripes had a black and white photo of Michigan Avenue in Chicago. Home sickness really struck me hard. Except for one furlough, I had been gone for almost two years. My future was really in limbo, nearing the age of twenty-five, I had no real hope of getting back into college. Without a trade or profession, my future was very uncertain. Some days I felt like a ship without a rudder. It is very difficult for a civilian to understand the complete isolation of a GI overseas. The thirteen month rotation policy in the military made it extremely difficult to make friends. Once the few you got to know well departed, the process had to start all over again. The fact that the Army functioned as well as it did is a testament to the flexibility of young American men and women. The mission was accomplished.

The Apollo circumnavigation of the moon in December 1968 was broadcast live in Korea. The narration was in Japanese, but we saw it as it happened. I do not know how the hookup was accomplished since there were no orbiting satellites in space at that time. I believe the signal was received from Australia and patched in through several stations in Vietnam, the Philippines, and Okinawa. It was an amazing technological feat in those days. The Korean people were in awe at the difficulty in getting men to the moon and viewed the event in absolute silence.

The failures of the Veteran's Administration in the post Vietnam period are well documented. Denial of Agent Orange benefits, understaffed medical facilities, delay in providing out-patient services, the list goes on. The current problems with the VA are now coming to light. The large number of PTSD patients are being treated in much the same manner as their predecessors were forty years ago. If a vet suffers from nightmares or sleeplessness sedate him. One victim of this protocol was recently on television. He held up a bag of over one hundred prescription medications he was taking each day. A team of pharmacologists could labor over the possible interactions of these pills for months and not come to a conclusion about their possible side effects. This is a scandal of the first order. The Iraq and Afghanistan wars were relatively small compared to Vietnam, yet the VA, now, seems overwhelmed by the number of Vets seeking help. What lessons were learned from previous conflicts about the treatment of traumatized veterans? Apparently, not many. The young marine receiving the pills said, "More men have died since their return from Afghanistan than were killed in combat." An investigation has been initiated in Chicago looking into the denial and delay of treatment by Hines hospital. Will the system ever change? During the Vietnam conflict the term "disposable veteran" came into vogue. Does history need to be repeated?

It took me years to realize that the policy initiated by General Bonesteel was correct. The Americans could help the Koreans in their battles with the guerillas, but, ultimately, it was theirs to win. The North Korean general responsible for the attempt to overthrow the government of Park Chung Hee was tried by Court Martial and shot. By the middle of 1969, hostilities ended. We had won. Few people are aware of what transpired on the peninsula between 1966-69. When I joined the VFW virtually no one in the local chapter was aware of the Second Korean War and they were reluctant to admit me. I came to the realization that a goodly number of the Vietnam vets had served on ships miles out in the Gulf of Tonkin, or were assigned to the many large base camps in country. They were referred to as REMF's (Rear echelon mother-fuckers). Those infantrymen who had seen combat, suffered from varying degrees of PTSD. Several were alcoholics. It seemed to me obscene that so much attention was being paid to

the POW/MIA issue. As of this writing, there are still black flags flying beneath the National Standard in thousands
of towns and villages across America in memory of missing Vietnam vets. More attention is being paid to the dead than the living. The final straw for me was a Christmas party a few years ago. My wife was greeted by a woman who chirped, "Merry Christmas if it is still all right to say it!" Ah yes, the mythic War on Christmas. A Fox news initiated fantasy that the secular humanists are out to destroy Christianity. I finally dropped out. I do not wish to denigrate this fine organization. They do wonderful work on behalf of veterans. Yet they seem oblivious to the fact that most programs for vets were initiated by Democratic presidents. FDR was responsible for the GI Bill of Rights after WWII. Millions of returning vets earned college degrees or graduated from trade schools as a result of this progressive legislation. My own Bachelor's and Master's degrees are largely due to the GI benefits accorded to Vietnam era vets. Why a preponderant number of veterans are Republicans continues to amaze me.

My last months overseas are a blur. I was no longer paying much attention to what was going on around me. I did my job which consisted of the usual TPR assessment of the patients and passing food trays. New people were placed on the extra duty roster. Keeping a low profile was advantageous when it came to scrutiny by the lifers. I saw Yobo one last time and said, "good bye". There were no tears or heartfelt farewells. She already seemed resigned to my departure and had moved on. The check-out procedure in the Army was an elaborate ritual. You were allowed to ship a box of souvenirs home courtesy of Uncle Sam. A senior enlisted man checked everything that went into the box. Mostly they were concerned with drugs and weapons. In Vietnam returning troops routinely attempted to ship home hand grenades, claymore mines, and drugs. One enterprising GI wanted to bring home a mortar with explosive rounds. He probably would have gotten away with it but an alert NCO noticed he was struggling with his duffel bag. He was ordered to empty its contents on the

floor. The airport was cleared until explosive ordnance people were called in to remove the evidence. Whatever
happened to this GI is unknown, but I am sure he didn't receive a medal. Henceforth duffel bags were checked with metal detectors.

I had purchased a reel to reel tape recorder, but little else. The wooden box passed muster and it arrived back in Chicago before its owner. Shortly before my departure a letter was given to me from the former company commander Captain Sideburns. It was a Letter of Commendation! It was laudatory; "I had made a meaningful contribution to the successful completion of the hospital's mission." If I had been recommended for a medal of honor, my surprise could not have been greater. This was no doubt "recompense" for my lack of promotion. I entered the Army as a buck private and left as one. The clerk in the arms room actually asked if I wanted to keep my helmet and down filled sleeping bag. I declined, not wanting to be accused, once again, of stealing government property. The clearance process involved going to Seoul to check out formally with 8th Army. I shared the jeep with a newly arrived physician who was fresh from the states and appeared eager to see his new home. "Out Processing" in the Army is practiced at both ends. Many forms had to be filled out in Korea and further paper work was necessary when I arrived at Ft. Lewis. The newly arrived physician was a large, good looking man. Both of us were jammed together in the back of a jeep. We got to talking. He had just completed his residency and was newly married with a small child. Being a General Surgeon, his residency was a lengthy one. It seemed sad that he had left a wife and young daughter stateside for thirteen months. Little did I realize that in less than two weeks he would be dead.

Chapter 14

March 9, 1969

The day dawned foggy and wet. I was being accorded a private jeep ride to Kimpo airfield. I was wearing my class A uniform for the first time in thirteen months. The jeep driver smiled at me and said, "Glad your DEROS finally arrived."

"Are you kidding?" was my reply.

"How long do you have to go?"

"Ten months," was his reply. The sun was just beginning to rise when we reached Kimpo Airfield. A DC-8 was being serviced on the field: the fabled red tail. We were ushered into the terminal and inspected by an NCO for correct uniforms. It seems some months earlier a Colonel had braced a homeward bound enlisted man who showed up in a rumpled uniform. The Colonel asked why his grooming and class A's were in such a state. The EM replied, "Hey, I am out of the Army!" The officer was not pleased with the answer. From that day onward, all troops were subject to a uniform inspection. If you did not pass muster, you would not board the jet. The reaction was immediate. The duty NCO checked me out closely, he decided my trousers needed pressing. I was told to remove my pants. I gave him no argument. A little Korean lady was close by with an ironing board. What a way to leave! Pants down upon arrival, pants off upon departure! We were further required to have our dog tags on and our identity cards in the breast pockets of our blouses. The thinking behind this measure was if the plane crashed our blackened corpses could be readily identified. We boarded the aircraft and waited for about forty-five minutes to complete the pre-flight check and top off the fuel. The trip to Japan took several hours. Upon landing at Narita the aircraft was fueled again for the long twelve hour flight to Seattle. For some reason, the ground crew entered the aircraft and squatted in the middle of the aisle and smiled at us. This was not a "Welcome to Japan" greeting, rather a smirking acknowledgement that the Americans were losing the war in Vietnam. The Asiatics were finally giving Uncle Sam a dose of his own medicine. It was another moment that I will never forget. The "Sons of Nippon" had never forgotten or forgiven the humiliation of defeat in WWII. An Air Force Major entered the plane and sat down in the empty seat next to me. The aircraft taxied away from the terminal and lined up for take-off.

We settled in for the long flight and I struck up a conversation with the Major. It turned out that he was a reserve officer in the Ohio Air National Guard. He had been called to active duty as a consequence of the Tet offensive. The Major had never flown over North Vietnam and was exclusively flying tactical support missions for the Army in the south. The man looked exhausted and pale. He was still wearing his flight suit which was heavily stained with perspiration. I was curious why he had not showered or changed into class As for the flight home. Apparently his experiences in Vietnam had shaken his resolve, his eyes appeared haunted. After a few hours of small talk he opened up. There had been some sort of mix-up with ground control and he dropped his bombs in the wrong place. I never found out whether he had served his entire tour overseas, or had been relieved. In any case, he evidenced some serious inner turmoil that was not yet resolved. The war had claimed another victim.

Flying into night, the cabin lights were turned off and the troops began to nod off. I never went to sleep. My six foot six inch frame did not fit comfortably into the small seat. I walked back and forth in the cabin trying not to bump into any of the dozing soldiers. I was very excited and anxious to set foot on American soil.

McChord Air Force base had a swale in the runway. The aircraft hit the tarmac hard and the pilot almost immediately reversed the engines. I was thrown forward against the seatbelt and then slammed back in my seat. Welcome home! We boarded busses for the short trip to Ft. Lewis.

The casual barrack was bare of any amenities; the bunks had no mattresses. Great! The enjoyable prospect of sleeping on steel springs! Nothing is too good for our returning heroes! We were given two meal tickets after we handed in our military files. The manila folder that I turned in was twice as thick as those held by other returnees. Everything that had transpired in Korea was apparently included in the envelope. How thoughtful of them to include my rap sheet replete with the multiple article 15s. We were ushered into an auditorium to hear yet another lecture on military etiquette. However, this is not what happened. Most of the five hundred or more overseas vets were clad in khaki, they had just arrived from Vietnam. Those of us from Korea, Okinawa, or Japan were attired in class A greens. When we were seated a regular Army Major marched up to the lectern and began to speak. He said, in part, "Men you have just returned from overseas and have participated in a conflict that is no longer supported by large numbers of Americans. You may be subject to harassment and verbal abuse when you leave here. There is one thing that should sustain you in the future. The nation you served will remember your sacrifice in the years to come. No one can ever take that away from you. A pamphlet will be distributed which will document the benefits all veterans are entitled to. We will try to expedite your separation which will take 24 to 48 hours. God bless and keep you! Good luck!" I was impressed by the Major's honesty. He addressed the heart of the matter.

A Staff Sergeant was sitting immediately to my right, he bore the hash marks of service on his sleeve that indicated many years of active duty I asked him, "What are you doing here with all the short timers? Aren't regular Army people entitled to a retirement ceremony?"

The Sergeant replied, "I am not retiring, just leaving the Army."

"What do you mean?" I said.

He concluded, "I am getting out after sixteen years, no retirement benefits. I am finished with the Army before Vietnam finishes me."

There was another group of men in an ante room. They kept to themselves and did not hear the Major's speech. I asked about why they were segregated from the rest of us. "Oh," replied a Sergeant, "Those people are receiving less than honorable discharges they are not entitled to any benefits." We moved out and went to the nearest mess hall. The Vietnam vets got a blue meal ticket, steak and eggs. The rest of us got white tickets: pork chops and lima beans.

In the sparse barrack, I could not fall asleep on the inner spring bunk, no pillows were supplied. The next day we were called in individually to turn in our ID cards and receive Honorable Discharges. Travel pay was provided and busses made the shuttle run to SeaTac airport. I arrived after dark and managed to get a midnight flight to New York which stopped in Chicago. By this time my neat uniform was wrinkled and I had not shaved in 72 hours. Five hours later I boarded the Red Eye and headed home. Chicago was cold, but the day was cloudless and the sky was blue. I picked up my duffel bag and boarded a shuttle bus for Chicago. No one even noticed me. I was already anonymous. I had not slept in four days. It was over.

EPILOGUE

My mother cried and embraced me when I entered the house. I had phoned her and announced that I had arrived safely at O'Hare field. A bus took me into the city and I boarded the Burlington Northern train for the trip to the suburbs. A commuter bus took me to within a mile of my house and I walked the remaining distance. The forms were on the table for application to the University of Illinois. About ten days after my arrival home a letter came from Tom Grimaldi. There had been another firefight on the DMZ and a helicopter had been dispatched from the 642 to evacuate the casualties, the wounded were loaded on the aircraft and it took off. Shortly thereafter it crashed, killing all aboard including the physician I had shared the jeep ride with. He had been in Korea less than two weeks. The 642 also lost its sole helicopter pilot: a Major. I was numb for about three days. My admission to the University was conditional. If I did not maintain a B average my academic career would be permanently ended. My dedication to completing a degree was commendable. Determined, I closeted myself in my bedroom and really worked hard. I graduated in 1971 at the ripe age of twenty-seven and received a Masters Degree in Education in 1977.

My career did not run smoothly. The fact that I had dropped out and resumed my academic career two years later was a "Mark of Cain". To compensate for my checkered academic career I worked very hard. I always felt that no matter how hard I applied myself failure always loomed in the future. The magic number in my life was six. Although I taught for thirty-three years, I never worked longer than six years at any given school. My friend Tom Grimaldi returned to the States in May1969. He had spent twenty-three months in Korea. He applied for his old job and was refused employment at a tire factory in Akron, Ohio. Tom had a nervous breakdown and spent six weeks in a Veteran's hospital. After recovery he completed college and spent the rest of his life as an RN in Texas. I wrote Yobo a letter in the summer of 1969. She responded with a missive requesting money. I understood. She had sacrificed for me. I married my wife in 1971 and we had two boys, both of whom completed college and married. I am now a grandfather of two.

I have returned in my dreams many times to the 642 Hospital. The thirteen months in Korea seemed like a lifetime. So much had happened in a brief period of time. In my teaching career, I seldom encountered former servicemen. Teachers in the main did not serve in the military. It is difficult for me to comprehend the fact that the North Koreans are as irrational in the

Twenty-First century as they were in the 1960's. The country is an economic basket case, barely able to feed its own people. The question is often asked, "Would you do it over again?" Yes, most definitely, but better. If the war had not been fought between 1950 and 1953, would the Korean people be better off? That is a question easy to answer.

Mrs. Kim's husband was a North Korean, his parents boarded a Navy LST and fled south from Hungnam in 1950. They hated the Communist regime and preferred the unknown to remaining in the North. The economic progress made in the South has been incredible since the war. They are much better off.

I had a recurrent dream for years, standing on a street or in bed when a giant vortex appeared over me. It attempted to suck me up, and I knew Korea was at the other end pulling me back. I said, "Not me please, it's all done with. I'm forty years old with a family." But the vortex kept pulling. I would wake up soaking wet. The dreams finally stopped.

ASCOM ceased to exist in the 1970s. Bupyong is now covered with apartment buildings and condominiums. The clubs were shut down as a consequence of the AIDS crisis in the 1980's.

In 2001 my wife and I attended a ceremony at Arlington National Cemetery to honor those men who lost their lives along the DMZ between 1966 and 1969. I was honored to be one of the former soldiers to read the names. It was a moving experience to meet some of the mothers and relatives of the dead. Now, at age seventy, the memories are there and will remain vivid to the end of my days.

Photos

Maj. Gen. Frank M. Izenour, commanding general, 2nd Inf. Div., presents Mrs. Bok Hee Kim (5,000 won ($16) for reporting a North Korean infiltrator who hid in her house Jan. 24, and to help pay for damages caused by the ensuing firefight which ended with the infiltrator being killed. Looking on is Yu Bong Sik, Paju County police chief. (USA)

2 Korean Women Rewarded For Turning in Red Agents

CAMP HOWZE, Korea (IO)— Two Korean women who experienced terror in helping to turn North Korean infiltrators hiding in their houses were thanked by the 2nd Inf. Div. Monday and presented with money to help repair their battle-damaged residences.

Maj. Gen. Frank M. Izenour, commanding general 2nd Inf. Div., gave Mrs. Bok Hee Kim of Chonhyon-myon, Paju County, 15,000 won at Camp Howze Div. Headquarters.

Mrs. Kim's home was damaged Jan. 24 when elements of the 1st Bn., 23d Inf. alerted by her sound, closed in upon and killed a North Korean infiltrator hiding in one of the rooms.

...infiltrator crept into his home and...

At the office of Yu Bong Sik, the Paju County chief of police, Lt. Col. Wilmot A. Hall, Div. G-5 (Civil Affairs), presented Mrs. Chung Ooi Kim of Kwang Tan Myon, with 15,000 won for also helping trap a Communist agent.

On Jan. 30, at about 10 p.m., an agent appeared at her house and demanded food and a place to rest. She, too, sent her son to alert a neighboring police unit, which surrounded the house during the night.

...the next morning, after...
...gotten away, the...
...e agent, in a...
...killed him.

From The Frontiersman – The Eighth Army newspaper

Rural scenes in Korea 1968

COMMANDER BUCHER talks with U.S. Ambassador Porter about his experiences during imprisonment. GEN Bonesteel looks on (at left).

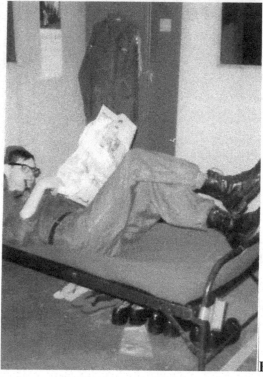

Barracks

Top: Me with Katusas on base. May 1968

Bottom : At Ft Sam Houston AIT, Sept-Oct 1967

Top : Thatching a roof in Korea

Bottom: Market in Bupyong

Bob Hope and Ann Margaret Christmas 1968

List of Terms

AK- Short for AK-47. Soviet main battle rifle. Also manufactured by China. .30 caliber. Deadly under 200 yards. 30 round magazine.

Ambu Bag- A rubber balloon with a valve used to introduce air into the lungs.

ASCOM- Large Base/Supply hub for Inchon and points north.

APC- M-113 Armored Personnel Carrier. Aluminum construction. Considered in Vietnam to be a death trap. Easily penetrated by a $20 B-40 rocket. Now obsolete.

CQ- Charge of Quarters. Generally a Buck Sergeant. Three Chevrons

DEROS- Time of Separation.   Departure for the United States

D.O.A. – Dead on arrival

Grease Gun- .45 Caliber sub-machine gun. Thirty round magazine. Replaced Thompson during WW11. Used extensively by ROK police.

Huey- Main work horse helicopter of Vietnam War. Carried troops or cargo.

KATUSA- Korean augmentation to the U.S. Army. Spoke some English. Generally educated.

JV- Short for Japanese village. High end prostitutes lived there. Frequented by officers.

M1 Carbine- Fired a pistol size .30 caliber cartridge. Used in WW11, Korea, and Vietnam. Range 100-150 yards

M-1 Garand Rifle- .30 Caliber. 8 round capacity. Used in WW11, Korea, and Vietnam. Accurate to 500 yards. Used by ROK army in Vietnam.

M-14 Rifle- The last wood and steel Army rifle. .30 Caliber, 20 round magazine. Accurate to 500 yards.

M-16 Rifle- .223 Caliber. Aluminum construction, adopted by the Army in 1965. Not noted for reliability in the 1960's. Aluminum magazine easily damaged. Had a 20 round magazine in 1968.

M2 Browning- .50 caliber belt feed machine gun. Very heavy 85 pounds. Used primarily on vehicles. Frequently used for static defense on DMZ.

M-79- Single shot 40mm grenade launcher. Now obsolete.

Navy AK- The Pueblo was an AK; a cargo ship converted to monitor radio traffic. Same type as seen in the movie "Mr. Roberts."

NCOIC- Non-commissioned officer in charge. Generally had some authority when officers were not available.

NKPA- North Korean People's Army.

O.D. – Officer of the Day

PFC- E-3 Private first class. Single chevron with attached rocker.

PPSH-43- Fired a .30 caliber pistol cartridge. Used by North Koreans in ambushes. A Soviet sub-machine gun used extensively
in WWII and Korea. Compact with a folding stock. Thirty round stick magazine.

PVT- E-2 Lowest enlisted rank. Single chevron.

ROK- Republic of Korea. In 1968 ruled by Dictator Park Chung Hee.

SFC- Sergeant First Class. Three chevrons up, two rockers down.

SSgt – Staff Sergeant

SOP – Standard Operating Procedure

Sp/4- E-4- A corporal without stripes. Wore a patch with American eagle.

Spec/5- E-5   Eagle patch with one rocker. Equal in pay grade to buck sergeant.

UNC- United Nations Command. Consisted mostly of ceremonial troops from the UK, Australia, and New Zealand. One large company from Thailand. Most of the   43,000 troops in Korea were American.

1st Sergeant- Three Chevrons up a diamond and two rockers.

.45 Colt-1911 A1- Standard automatic pistol of WW1, WW2, Korea, and Vietnam. Seven round capacity. Deadly at close range. Replaced in 1980's by 9mm Beretta.

.

Made in USA - Kendallville, IN
78969_9781505636000
08.26.2022 1426